THUMB INDEX →

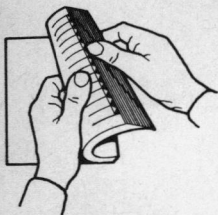

This book is arranged alphabetically with a thumb index so that you can find the information you want in a few seconds. In addition, there is a glossary of parts and terms and a full index at the end of the book.

Introduction to Bicycles
TYPES · SIZE · BUYING

Accessories
BELLS · KICKSTANDS · EXTRAS

Baby Seats
TYPES · CARRYING A CHILD

Baskets and Carriers
CHOOSING · TYPES

Brakes
TYPES · ADJUSTING · FIXING

Chain Drive
ON 1- AND 3-SPEED BIKES

Children's Bikes
TYPES · SIZE · BUYING

City Riding
SURVIVING IN TRAFFIC

Clothing
FOR WARMTH, RAIN, SAFETY

Frames
CONSTRUCTION · FORKS

Gears — Derailleur
USING · ADJUSTING · FIXING

Gears — 3-speed
USING · ADJUSTING

Gear Numbers and Speed
EXPLAINED · TABLES

CONTINUED AT BACK

For Barbara

WARNER PAPERBACK LIBRARY EDITION

Text designed by
Don Earnest

First Printing: March 1973
Second Printing: October 1973

Original illustrations by
Reproduction Drawings Ltd

Warner Paperback Library
is a division of
Warner Books, Inc.
75 Rockefeller Plaza,
New York, N.Y. 10019

Cover photograph by
Paul Weller

The Backpocket Bicycle Book

by
Don Earnest

WARNER
PAPERBACK
LIBRARY

A Warner Communications Company

Introduction

Perhaps it was because it resembled a horse—as the name hobby horse applied to one of its earliest ancestors suggests—but it is amazing that anyone should have thought of it. A pedaled tricycle and a pedaled cart were predictable, but putting two wheels in a line was an unlikely combination if there ever was one. It probably would be condemned as unstable by a Federal safety board if it were introduced today. But people took to the bicycle. It was probably because of the greater freedom it offered—even if it meant learning to balance on two thin wheels. The early cyclist discovered that he had almost as much freedom of movement and freedom to go where he wanted as the walker, with the advantage that he could go further faster. When it was finally perfected in a safe, mass-produced form in the 1890's, the bicycle was, literally, a vehicle of liberation. For those who didn't own a horse, it was the first means for the individual to get around quickly, to see the countryside, to go where he wanted and not just where the train took him. Some people maintain, as its early critics feared, that it was partly responsible for more social freedom: taking couples out from under the watchful eyes of their elders and freeing women from the cumbersome clothes of the 19th century. A few writers even go so far as to ascribe a social revolution to the introduction of the bicycle.

That initial sense of freedom has remained with the bicycle. It was the secret of those adults who persevered with it during the years of its eclipse by the automobile, when it was relegated to the position of a child's toy. Although many people dismissed them as eccentrics, they were a hardy, individualist group who pedaled their way to a healthy old age.

Today, when people feel increasingly cut off from their senses, more and more people are seeking ways to get back in touch with the world. Much has been written about

4

how good cycling is for you—about how it is one of the best unregimented and practical means of keeping fit, losing weight, and avoiding heart attacks. But it is more likely that the reason so many people have again taken up cycling is that, after one taste of it, they have found that it is a great way to restore feeling to their deadened senses. For those who are used to sealing themselves in heavy metal shells when they travel, it can be a sensuous experience. They are unencumbered and free. They are moving under their own power, using their muscles actively, not being carried along passively. Their senses are not cut off: they can hear, smell, and feel the rush of wind. They are going fast enough to feast their senses but can easily stop to savor a detail. The psychological benefits are probably as great as the physical ones.

Some are discovering another secret about the bike—it is a practical, economical way to get around. It doesn't require fuel. It rarely needs major repairs, and it is such a simple machine that the occasional minor repairs can be handled by most riders. In the city, it is often faster than a car, and it can be parked almost anywhere.

A word of warning to those who don't know it already: cycling is habit forming—dependency often lasts well into the eighties. You will feel cooped up, cramped, and often ill in a car. A marked irritability and fidgeteness may develop if you go too long without riding. You'll curse rainy, snowy, or windy days when you can't take your bike, and you may end up soaked or frostbitten to avoid getting on a slow, crowded, stale-smelling bus. You'll make excuses to use your bike, just to get some air. As dependence increases, you'll find yourself taking longer and longer trips. When you become totally addicted, you will have trouble walking when you get off your bike because you have been pedaling so long. If you get on a bike just once, you can become hooked for life.

Types of Bicycles

All modern bicycles are direct descendants of the "Safety Bike" of 1885, which replaced an amazing variety of now extinct two-wheel vehicles with pedals, including the popular but dangerous high-wheelers. And most of the differences between the types of modern bikes are a matter of weight, gearing, styling, and quality.

Bikes weigh from 20 to 50 pounds. The importance of weight can be understood if you consider that the lighter the bike is the less you have to propel with your muscles —and the longer the ride the more important every pound saved will be. But for every pound you don't pedal, the cost of the bike goes up. And there is always some loss of strength when weight is saved, although on better bikes it is usually compensated for by better engineering.

The number of "speeds" or gears a bike has—and their range—is also important for reducing the effort required to pedal, especially on hills. On bikes with variable gears, you can change the distance you travel with each pedal turn and with it, the effort needed to pedal. But the more gears a bike has, the more skill that is needed to use them and the more care they need.

Styling is not just a matter of appearance. The style of seat, pedals, and tires affects your riding efficiency and comfort. And the shape of the handlebars affects the entire way that you ride a bike—whether you assume a casual upright position or a forward racing position.

Quality is determined by the precision of the engineering of the moving parts and the construction of the frame. In general, price is a good relative indication of quality, but the price of the same bike can vary by as much as 25 percent from one store to another, and prices increase geometrically in the upper ranges for racing-quality workmanship. Only the relative differences in prices between types of bikes are indicated here because no exact prices would be valid for more than a few months.

Buying and size: If you are interested in buying a bike, you should be able to choose the kind that suits your needs from the descriptions on the following pages. But there are other factors to consider when you are looking for a bike, and the most important is the size of the bike.

The size of a bike is determined by both the size of the wheels and of the frame. But since most adult bikes come with wheels either 26 or 27 inches in diameter, you don't need to worry about wheel size unless you are so tall or short that one inch matters. Frame size, however, makes a big difference in riding comfort and efficiency.

The frame size of a bike is measured along the length of the seat tube from its top, where the seat post enters it, to the center of the pedal crank (see p. 42). On adult bikes, this length varies from around 17 to 26 inches. Not all sizes are available on all bikes or in all stores, but you should get a bike with a frame size from 12 to 13 inches less than the length of your leg, measured from the crotch to the heel of the shoe. This gives you enough flexibility to adjust the seat height. On bikes with men's frames, be sure you can straddle the top tube comfortably with both feet on the ground.

On folding bikes, you don't need to be concerned about frame size since they can be adjusted over a wide range.

It is a good idea to ride a bike you are thinking of buying to see if it feels right and if anything is wrong with it. But remember that you have to get used to some bikes —especially if you are switching from a bike with conventional features to one with racing features. In general, buying a bike at a bike store where you can try it out and where it will be assembled, adjusted, and checked out for you will avoid frustration and save time, but not money. A crated bike from a department store is the alternative. Use the maintenance guide on pp. 88–93 to check out a new or used bike.

English (3-speed) Bikes

These bikes are commonly called "English racers" or "tourist" bikes, although they are not made only in England, are not racing bikes, and are not ideal for long tours. But they are good everyday bikes for getting around the city, for trips in the neighborhood, for weekend pleasure riding, and even for short day excursions. And in many areas they have become the standard bike for adults.

Today, nearly every bike manufacturer makes at least one version of the English bike. They vary in quality and price from plush expensive models to second-line models to cheap grade-C models. The difference between the cheapest models and the better models is primarily in frame construction—the better models have stronger, better joined, better finished frames. Between the expensive and the second-line models, however, the differences are often in the quality of the other parts, the number of accessories, and the name. The expensive ones are likely to have features such as leather seats, carriers, and built-in hub generators. But nearly all models with reasonable care and occasional overhauls should give years of casual riding. And none are very expensive—the ones at the upper end overlap in price with the cheaper derailluer bikes.

Although they are usually advertised as "lightweights," they weigh from 35 to 40 pounds, which is about as heavy as an adult who rides much should consider. They have conventional features: mattress (or loop-spring) seats, raised handlebars, rubber pedals, and full fenders. And they are designed to be ridden in an almost upright position, which most people consider "normal" and prefer for leisurely riding. They nearly always have 26-inch wheels with medium-pressure tires, $1\frac{3}{8}$ inches wide, which give a softer, more stable ride than the narrower

tires on most derailleur bikes. And they usually have hand-operated brakes with levers on the handlebars connected by cables to front and rear wheel caliper units which grasp the rim of the wheel when you brake. These are the side-pull type of brakes and they require occasional adjustment.

The gears on these bikes, which are inside the hub of the rear wheel, are called "hubchanger" or "hub" gears. They are easy to use and are controlled by a small trigger unit, or a twist grip, on the handlebars with click stops. Although some expensive models come with 4- and 5-speed hub gears, most models come with 3-speed gears. The three gears or "speeds" are low, normal, and high. The low gear (L or 1) is for climbing hills, for going against a strong wind, or for carrying a load. The normal gear (N or 2) is for riding on a level surface. And the high gear (H or 3) is for gaining speed, especially going downhill. (For more on hub gears, see p. 62.) The low gear is sufficient to get you over small hills with a little extra effort, but a lot of extra effort is required for a fairly steep or long hill. If you live in a hilly area, you will probably be better off with a derailleur bike.

Derailleur Bikes

Derailleur bikes vary greatly in weight, quality, and price, and since many of them look alike, it's often hard to tell them apart.

What they all have in common are derailleur gears— an external method of changing the gear ratio between the pedals and the back wheel. At the rear of these bikes, where the chain drives the back wheel, there is a cluster of five chain sprockets of increasing size and a device that the chain passes through which moves it from sprocket to sprocket when you move the gear shift lever. When the chain changes sprockets, the speed of the back wheel, relative to your pedaling, changes. And the effort needed to pedal also changes. If a bike only has a rear multiple sprocket, it's a 5-speed. One gear is attained on each of the five rear sprockets. But if a bike has two sprockets and another, simpler changer at the pedal end of the chain, it's a 10-speed since with two front and five rear sprockets, ten combinations are possible. And if it has three sprockets in the front, it's a 15-speed.

In use, the difference between a 5-speed and a 10-speed is that the 10-speed offers much more flexibility in gearing—in effect, a gear to meet every condition: hills, wind, load, and physical condition. The changes on the 5-speed are much more abrupt. And since a 10-speed of comparable quality costs little more, 10-speeds are a better buy. Fifteen-speeds are recommended only if you travel in mountainous areas. Since derailleur gears are exposed, they require more care, and using them effectively is a skill. (For more on gears, see p. 46).

Derailleur bikes differ in the construction of the frame and the quality of the parts. Although you have to be careful because there are some poor quality, cheap ones on the market, most of these bikes fall into three groups: good, better, and best.

Good everyday 5- and 10-speed derailleur bikes are one step up from 3-speeds—primarily in gearing. The frame is the same or very nearly the same as the ones on 3-speeds. As a result, the bike weighs about the same— in the 35 to 40 pound range. And although about half of the men's models come with dropped handlebars, racing seats, metal pedals, and no fenders, most of the women's models and the rest of the men's have conventional seats and handlebars and full fenders. But the wheels are usually the larger 27-inch ones with the narrower high-pressure tires, 1¼ inches wide, which give a faster but harder ride with less road resistance. The gears, which give the bike its great advantage over the 3-speed, are often the less expensive, sturdy ones that were designed originally for children's high-rise bikes and they can withstand a lot of abuse. On some bikes, however, they are of poor quality and may break with rigorous use. But it doesn't cost too much to replace them.

These bikes are fine for casual riding and are a good compromise for people who need good gearing and want conventional styling. They cost more than 3-speeds, but in a hilly area they are worth it. They can be used for touring, but they are not as ideal as the lighter bikes.

Better 10-speeds are often the second or third line of companies whose top line is professional road racing bikes. They are mass produced, but cost from one and a half to three times more than the less expensive 10-speeds. And they are about as good a bike as the average rider needs and probably can afford. The frames are made of a stronger alloy steel—usually a chrome alloy but sometimes the even better manganese alloy. As a result, the tubes can be thinner and the weight of the bike drops to under 30 pounds. But unlike the top line, the frame tubes are not thicker at stress points, and the use of aluminum alloy to further reduce weight is limited to the handlebars, the hubs, and sometimes the rims. Nearly all have a diamond-shaped men's frame, dropped handlebars, racing seat, metal pedals, and no fenders. A few women's models are made with a mixte frame (see p. 44), flat handlebars, and fenders. All have 27-inch wheels, most with $1\frac{1}{4}$-inch conventional tires. The hand brakes are usually the center-pull type that give more even braking and need less attention than side-pulls. The hubs and brakes usually have quick-release levels so the wheels can be removed easily for repair. The gears are of good quality and have a wide range.

The best 10- and 15-speeds available, short of getting a custom-built bike, are road-racing models. And they are designed for racing, not for average cyclists. Everything has been done to reduce the weight and increase the speed potential of these bikes. The frames are made of manganese-molybdenum steel alloy tubing. This tubing, which nearly always bears the brand name Reynolds 531 or Columbus, has a high tensile strength and is very thin. And for more strength, the tubes are "butted" —slightly thicker at the joints. Most of the other metal components are made of aluminum alloy for lightness— rims, hubs, cranks, brakes, gears, handlebars, and sprockets. The 27-inch wheels have special shallow rims for the very narrow racing tires called "tubulars" or "sew-ups." The result is a bike under 25 pounds.

Although the frame is stronger, these bikes are not as utilitarian as the second-line bikes because of the extensive use of aluminum alloy. This material is much softer than steel, and to reduce the wear on the moving parts they are precision made. To keep them from wearing out, they require frequent overhauls and precise adjustment. The hubs alone can cost more than a new 3-speed to replace. Care in riding is also necessary to avoid bending these soft alloy parts.

The derailleur gears are the best quality made, but they usually have a close and fairly high range since they are intended to be used for speed by strong riders. But the range can be altered by replacing the sprockets.

The brand name Campagnolo on the gears, brakes, hubs, and even the dropouts that hold the wheel is a sign of quality, but other good brands are made.

These are fine machines, not to be knocked around, left in the rain, or even chained to a lamp post unless you can afford to replace one. They are only for serious cyclists who are willing to care for them.

Folding Bikes

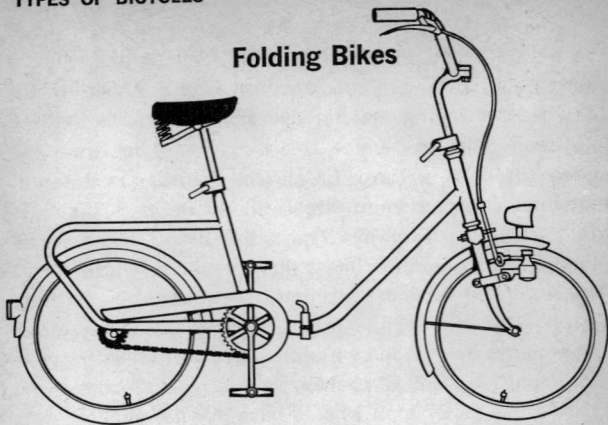

In the few years since they were introduced, the small-wheeled folding bikes have become popular for their non-riding advantages—their compactness and portability when folded. Except for a few with telescoping frame tubes, most have an open frame with a large, hinged-down tube, folding handlebars, and telescoping seat and handlebar posts. Most models can be collapsed by flicking a few levers. But they are quite heavy—around 40 pounds for most models—which limits their portability and rideability. Part of this weight often comes from a built-in rear carrier and other accessories such as generator lights. The small 16- or 20-inch wheels with wide low-pressure tires add to their compactness, but make them less stable and more tiring to steer than other bikes.

There are single-speed models with coaster brakes and 3-speed models with hand brakes. And the gear ratio on both is relatively low to compensate for the weight.

Basically these are short-range bikes, good for people who never travel far and have storage problems. But for their weight and quality, they are expensive, although the price has been dropping recently because of competition.

Others

Middleweights were the standard American bike until 20 years ago, but now most of the ones sold, even the 26-inch wheel models, are for children—although an adult can ride one. They have no gears, pedal-operated coaster brakes, wide low-pressure "balloon" tires, and heavy durable frames, which can be identified by their curved tubes. They are simple, sturdy, and require little maintenance—which makes them ideal for children. But they are the heaviest bikes made and are suitable only for short neighborhood trips. They can handle rough road surface better than other bikes.

Adult tricycles are middleweight in construction, with an open (woman's) frame. Most have small 20- or 24-inch wheels with wide tires, and some models can be folded. They are available in both single-speed and 3-speed models. Although they are expensive compared to bikes and not practical in traffic, they are excellent in resorts and retirement communities and are useful for shopping.

Tandems are bicycles built for two (or more). Most have a heavy middleweight frame and are not very useful for anything but once around the park. Better ones with lightweight construction and good gearing are also made and are fun for a pair of skilled riders. But with all models, for the price you can get two bikes of equal quality. The only practical use for a tandem is for touring—when an adult can ride with a child who would not normally be able to undertake the trip. But the tandem has to have a short rear seat tube.

Track bikes are designed for cycle track racing. They are basically the same as the best road racing derailleur bikes except that they have no gears or brakes, must be pedaled constantly, and weigh around 20 pounds.

Accessories

None of the accessories covered here* are necessary for riding, and many experienced riders don't use them because they feel that they add weight, break easily, or create a false sense of safety. They also know that an uncluttered bike is easier to ride and easier to fix. But if you decide you want any of these, a wide variety is available at any place that carries bicycle supplies. The inexpensive ones tend to go quickly, either from use or weather. A couple of thin coats of a clear, aerosol spray enamel on chromed parts is recommended to help prevent rust. For children just beginning to ride, these accessories, except kickstands, are distracting and therefore possibly dangerous.

A bell or horn is required by law in many areas and you may feel safer with one, but it is not safe to rely too much on one to warn today's sealed cars of your presence. They are good for warning pedestrians, but remember pedestrians have the right of way anyway. If you get a bell or horn, get a loud one; a tiny bell or weak one-cell horn is worse than nothing. A loud bicycle bell is probably the best because the sound it produces is one that most people immediately associate with a bicycle. It is small and compact, and a good one will last for years. Battery-operated horns vary in quality and loudness, but even with the best of them you have to remember to change the batteries. If you forget to take them out when you store your bicycle, for example, during the winter, they can corrode and ruin the horn. This can happen even when you're using your bike and forget about them for a long time. Bulb horns come in every possible shape and pitch, but they are really playthings that take up a lot of space. Whistles and sirens are illegal in most states.

* Also see: For baby seats, p. 18; for baskets and carriers, p. 20; for lights and reflectors, p. 78; for locks, p. 80; and for tools, p. 86.

A kickstand can be very handy and sometimes necessary, although it does add weight. The most common type is the fold-up side leg that attaches between the chain stays just behind the pedaling mechanism. (On many bikes it is built in.) If you get one, be very sure to get the right size; it should hold your bike at about a 75 to 80 degree angle from the ground. A much greater or lesser angle and your bike will crash over just from the wind. Another type of kickstand, called a Trygg or "trick" stand, has two legs and holds a bike upright with one wheel slightly off the ground. It is more stable and is useful when you are making repairs. A good kickstand should have a strong spring, which may make it "stiff" and hard to use at first. The bolt that holds a kickstand needs to be tightened occasionally, but be sure not to tighten it so hard that you damage the chain stays, which are irreplaceable.

A mileage meter, also called an odometer or cyclometer, is a small, inexpensive, but noisy device that attaches to the fork or seat stays. It measures the miles covered to the nearest tenth or hundredth by counting the revolutions of the wheel. Be sure to get the right one for your wheel size and mount as directed. It should be checked frequently since it can vibrate loose. And if one falls into your spokes, you can be thrown from your bike.

A rearview mirror is a mixed blessing. It does show you what's behind you, but it breaks easily, reflects sun in your eyes, and can be dangerous in case of an accident. Mount it on the left since you usually ride on the right side of the road.

A speedometer, even the most expensive, is not very reliable, breaks easily, and puts a drag on your wheel. (To calculate your average speed, see p. 71.)

Baby Seats
and Carrying a Child

A child can be safely carried on a baby seat from age one until five or six. The recommended stopping point is when the child weighs 40 pounds. But carrying 30 or 35 pounds of extra weight for any distance requires a strong and experienced rider.

The problem is not just the extra weight. Carrying any load high up on your bike makes it top heavy. Thus, many nervous parents have found their first experience disconcerting. If you have never ridden with a load on your bike, try riding with something other than your child a few times to get the feel of balancing the weight. When you do ride with your child, take it easy, use a low gear if you have one, and avoid traffic and hilly terrain until you feel completely confident. Even after you have become experienced at riding with a child, you should be more careful than usual. Avoid sudden or jerky movements. Be especially careful not to turn a corner too sharply or quickly. Slow down even more than usual when you turn and make a wide almost upright turn. If your bike has gears, you'll find it much easier if you use a lower gear as your normal riding gear on level terrain. On a three-speed this won't leave you with a hill-climbing gear, so you may want to have all of your gears lowered by getting a larger rear sprocket (see p. 64). If your bike doesn't have gears, avoid steep hills. With a child on the back, it's hard to get off and walk your bike up the hill when you can't make it. On any bike, you need a little extra air in the tire carrying the load.

On cool days, remember that a child, who is not pedaling the way you are, will feel the cold much more than you and should be more warmly dressed. When the temperature drops into the forties, it is too cold to ride a child except for short distances.

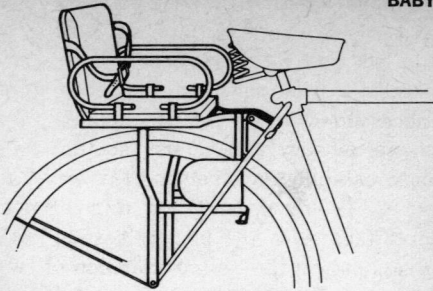

Rear child carriers are the best. And the ones that fold up (shown above) are better than the molded plastic ones because they can be used as a carrier when you are not carrying a child. But whichever type you get, be sure it has side arms, footrests, and most important of all, foot shields to keep the child's feet out of the spokes. Since a rear child carrier mounts directly on the rear axle, it makes it difficult to remove the back wheel and may, if you carry a child who's too heavy, damage the axle threads. The footrests on some models limit pedaling and have to be avoided when you are getting on and off.

Front child carriers, which mount on the handlebars, have the advantage that you can see and talk to your child. But the extra weight on the handlebars makes steering difficult, and their use should be limited to children under 30 pounds. Also, they can only be used on bikes with conventional handlebars since they make the forward-riding position used with dropped bars almost impossible.

Any baby seat should have a safety belt. If you buy a seat without one, you can make one out of an old belt. For children under three, use a full child's harness.

The small seats that mount on the top tube of the frame are not recommended because they don't mount securely, and carrying a child in this position interferes with pedaling and steering.

Baskets and Carriers

Most cyclists find that they need some type of carrier, and there is a wide selection to choose from. But like other accessories, most are of middling to poor quality and are a heavy and clumsy addition to your bike. So choose carefully, and get one that suits your needs, fits your bike, and doesn't add a great deal of extra weight unnecessarily. It's usually best to get the smallest and lightest carrier—or combination of carriers—you can get away with. Of course, if you use your bike primarily for shopping, then you'll need large roomy baskets.

Getting a carrier to fit your bike is important. Make sure that any carrier with supports is right for your wheel size, and in the case of a supported front basket, for your handlebar height too. Most narrow carriers will only fit one wheel size and many won't fit on a very large or small frame. If you have a folding bike without a built-in carrier, you may have trouble finding a carrier to fit it.

Also make sure that the carrier doesn't damage your bike or interfere with its operation. Any carrier that is supported directly on the axle of a wheel can damage the axle threads. An unsupported front basket, if you put much weight in it, can pinch and wear out your brake cables. On dropped handlebars, a front basket will greatly limit your hand positions. And rear saddle baskets can interfere with pedaling and will limit your maneuverability in traffic.

If you do ride with a heavy load, balance it from front to back—and from side to side with saddle baskets. And remember, your bike will handle differently, so take it easy and avoid making sharp turns.

Bike trailers are made but they are heavy, expensive, and not practical for most cyclists. They are much too heavy for touring and not safe in traffic.

Touring equipment is discussed on p. 127.

Narrow spring-clip carriers are the best all-round carriers, and the light aluminum ones don't add much weight. But their use is limited to regular-shaped, not easily squashed objects, such as books, briefcases, and boxes, and except for small objects, you need a luggage strap to hold things on securely. Both front and back ones are made. Pannier (saddle) bags can be attached to them for touring.

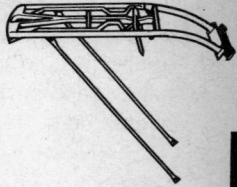

Wire saddle baskets can carry a lot and carry it in a stable, low position. But they are heavy and bulky, can interfere with pedaling, and make it difficult to change the back wheel. Most are one unit, but you can get baskets that clip onto a rear carrier.

Woven front baskets are small and easily attached by straps but are only good for very light loads—a purse, a small sack, or a sweater.

Wire front baskets can be attached securely, are well supported, and can carry a heavy load. But too heavy a load makes steering difficult, and the baskets themselves are a heavy dead weight when you are not using them.

Small seat-attached bags are called "touring bags" but their capacity is so limited that even for casual riding they are a minimal carrier. The even smaller tool bags are useful, but, left on your bike, your tools may be stolen.

Brakes

Two types of brakes are commonly used on bicycles: hand-operated rim brakes, found on nearly all adult bikes with gears, and pedal-operated coaster brakes, found on children's bikes and adult bikes without gears. Sometimes a bike with coaster brakes will have a supplementary hand brake on the front wheel. Coaster brakes are discussed on p. 29, and braking on p. 103.

Hand-operated Rim Brakes

A quick look at your bike will show you how rim brakes work. For each wheel, there is a lever on the handlebars that is connected by a cable to a stirrup-shaped device that the tire passes through. This device is the rim brake. It is also known as a "caliper brake," although it acts more like a pair of tongs than a caliper. When you squeeze the lever, the pull on the cable causes the arms of the brake to pivot together and grab the rim of the wheel. Each brake arm has a small block of rubber— called a "brake shoe"—and it is the friction between the rubber shoes and the metal rim that stops the wheel. When you let go of the lever, the brake springs open.

Rim brakes give good braking, allowing you either to slow the bike down gradually or to bring it to a sudden stop—depending on how much pressure you apply to the hand levers. But they won't hold when the rim is wet, and on rainy days you have to ride very carefully.

All rim brakes work on the same principle, but there are two types of rim units and two types of levers. They are illustrated on the following pages.

Side-pull rim brakes are the most common and are used on nearly all 3- and 5-speed bikes and on many 10-speeds. On these units, the cable pulls from one side, and the brake arms are joined by one pivotal bolt, which is also the bolt that holds the brake onto the frame. It can be tricky to adjust this bolt so that it is tight enough to keep the unit solidly attached and at the same time loose enough to let the arms move freely. As a result of the side pull and the single pivotal bolt, these brakes often go out of adjustment and give uneven braking.

Center-pull rim brakes are used on better lightweights. On these brakes, a short secondary cable, called a "transverse cable" runs between the brake arms and is pulled from above by the main cable (forming an inverted Y). There are two pivotal bolts, one for each arm, plus a mounting bolt. As a result, the unit brakes more evenly and requires less frequent adjustment.

Hand levers are all simple devices for pulling the cables. And the type will usually depend on the kind of handlebars. Raised handlebars have conventional, or "tourist," hand levers. Dropped handlebars have racing-style levers, often called "hooded" levers because of the rubber hood that usually covers the lever post. Some racing-style lever units have an extra, longer lever that can be grabbed when the hands are on the center of the handlebars. The most important thing about brake levers is their position, and they should always be mounted where they can be reached easily—even if moving them requires untaping and retaping dropped handlebars.

Maintenance: All rim brakes need to be readjusted occasionally because some part has worked loose or been hit. It is important that the shoes touch the rim and not the tire, which could cause a blowout. Eventually, the cable will go and the brake shoes will wear out. These are easy to fix. But other replacement parts are hard to find, and if the bike is treated roughly, a lever, a pivotal bolt, or a brake arm can be bent, and the entire unit probably will have to be replaced. Adjustments are on the following pages. A trouble-shooting chart is given on p. 28.

Rim Brake Units

Note: The brake shoes should be positioned so that they are $\frac{1}{8}''$ to $\frac{3}{16}''$ from rim and aligned with it.

To move brake shoes in or out: Loosen lockring. Screw adjusting sleeve out to move shoes closer to rim. Screw it in to move them away from rim. If this doesn't move them enough, adjust the cable tension. On some bikes, the brake shoes are on rods which can be moved in or out.

To release brakes: While holding the cable end to keep it from sliding through, loosen the anchor bolt. On center-pull brakes, the transverse cable usually can be released on the unanchored end, if you are only adjusting hand levers or removing the wheel. Also, some bikes have a quick-release lever next to the adjusting sleeve or a lever or button on the hand lever for this purpose.

To adjust cable tension: Loosen lockring and screw adjusting sleeve in all the way. Loosen anchor bolt. Then, while holding both shoes against the rim (tie if necessary), pull the cable taut and tighten anchor bolt. Adjust cable sleeve.

To replace brake shoes: Unscrew brake-shoe nut and old shoe will come off. Insert new shoe with closed metal end to the front of the bike, align with rim, and replace nut. You can replace just the rubber pad, but it's more difficult and not much cheaper. Always replace both shoes.

To adjust pivotal bolt on side-pull unit: This bolt is tricky to adjust. Throughout adjustment, keep the unit centered.

If <u>bolt</u> has <u>acorn</u> <u>nut</u> and locknut, make sure the nut on the frame side is tight. Then, loosen acorn nut and tighten locknut against unit. Back it off a half-turn, test brakes, and move it in or out as needed. Then, holding locknut to keep it from turning, tighten acorn nut against it.

If <u>the</u> <u>pivotal</u> <u>bolt</u> <u>has</u> <u>a</u> <u>slotted</u> <u>head</u> (like a screw), hold nut on the frame side with a wrench to keep it from turning and tighten the bolt with a screwdriver. Then, back off a half-turn, test brakes, and move bolt in or out as needed.

To adjust center-pull brakes: First, make sure unit is centered and mounting bolt is tight. Then, both pivotal bolts should be tightened and backed off a half-turn. Test brakes and move pivotal bolts in or out as necessary.

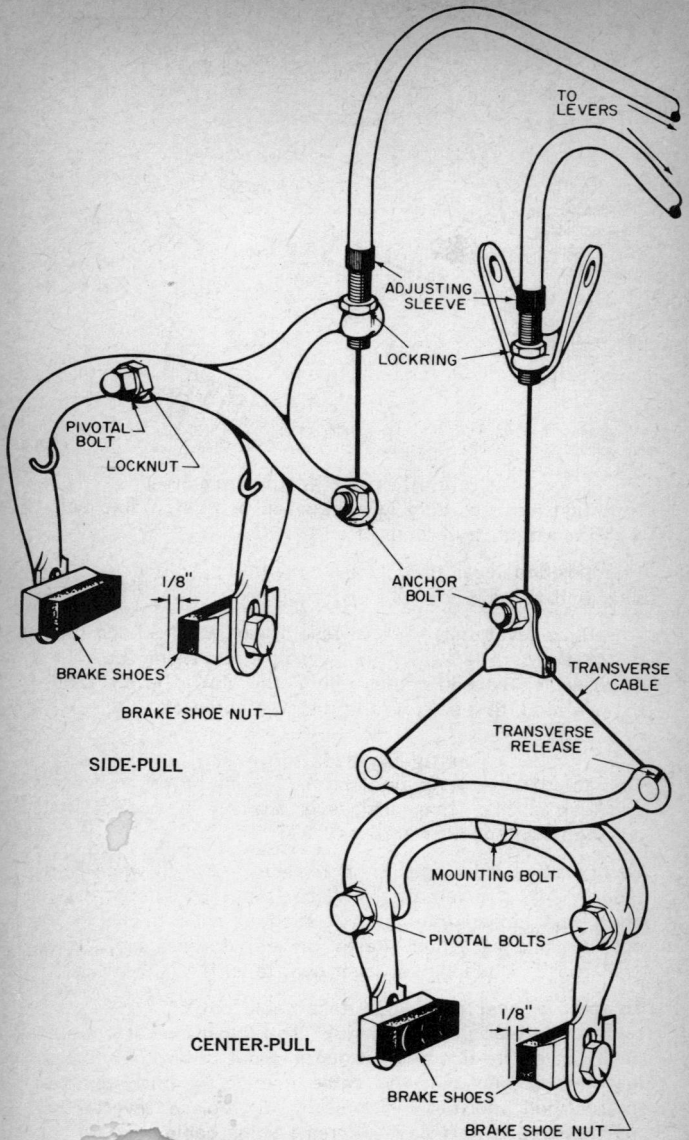

TO LEVERS

ADJUSTING SLEEVE

LOCKRING

PIVOTAL BOLT

LOCKNUT

ANCHOR BOLT

1/8"

BRAKE SHOES

BRAKE SHOE NUT

SIDE-PULL

TRANSVERSE CABLE

TRANSVERSE RELEASE

MOUNTING BOLT

PIVOTAL BOLTS

BRAKE SHOES

1/8"

CENTER-PULL

BRAKE SHOE NUT

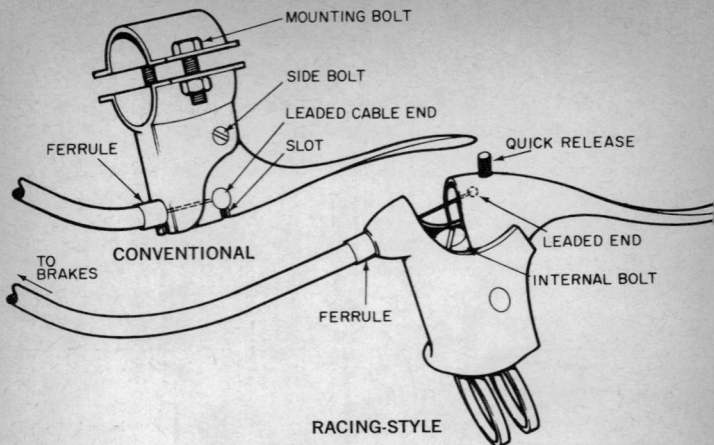

Diagram labels (clockwise): MOUNTING BOLT, SIDE BOLT, LEADED CABLE END, QUICK RELEASE, SLOT, LEADED END, INTERNAL BOLT, FERRULE, RACING-STYLE, FERRULE, CONVENTIONAL, TO BRAKES

Conventional Hand Levers

To adjust loose or tight lever: Loosen or tighten side bolt. If still too tight, try a drop of oil.

To reposition lever unit: Loosen mounting bolt(s) slightly, slide unit to new position, and retighten.

To remove lever unit: First, release brakes at wheel end (see p. 24). Pull ferrule away from lever post and swing the cable down so leaded end comes out of the slot in lever. Then, remove mounting bolt(s), and unit will come off.

Racing-Style Hand Levers

To tighten loose lever unit: First, release brakes at wheel end (see p. 24). Then, push lever down to expose internal bolt and tighten. Reset brakes.

To reposition lever unit: First, release brakes at wheel end (see p. 24), and remove handlebar tape. Then, push lever down and loosen internal bolt slightly. Slide unit to new position and retighten. Reset brakes. Retape handlebars (see p. 75). Don't mount lever over tape; it's not safe.

To remove lever unit: First, take cable out of anchor bolt on rim unit (see previous page). Then, push lever down and push cable wire in to get leaded end out of lever. Grab the leaded end and pull the cable completely out. Remove internal bolt and unit will come off. To replace, reverse the procedure. See next page for reattaching cable.

Cables

To adjust cable tension: See p. 24.

To replace cable: You can choose to replace the cable wire alone or both the wire and its housing (the tubing the cable wire goes through). There is no need to replace the housing unless it is damaged. Examine it carefully, and if it looks worn or kinked, see the note below and replace it as you go along. The new cable wire should be the same thickness (or slightly smaller), same length (or longer), and have the same leaded end as the old one. Don't cut it until after it's mounted; it's hard to get cut strands through the housing and the anchor bolt.

1 Detach cable wire at wheel end by loosening the anchor bolt (see p. 25).

2 On <u>conventional</u> <u>hand</u> <u>lever</u>, pull ferrule away from the lever post, swing the cable down, and push the leaded end out of the lever. Pull wire out of housing. Then, put new cable wire through ferrule and housing (a light coat of grease helps). Reseat leaded end in lever and ferrule in the lever post.

On <u>racing-style</u> <u>levers</u>, push lever down and push cable wire in to get it out of the slot in the lever. Grab the leaded end of the wire and pull it out. Then, thread the new cable wire through the hole in the lever post, then through the ferrule and the housing (a light coat of grease helps). Reseat leaded end in slot in the lever.

3 At wheel end, thread cable wire through the hole in the anchor bolt and adjust cable tension as described on p. 24.

New cables stretch and will need to be readjusted later.

If housing is also being replaced: New housing should be compatible with the new cable wire and old ferrule(s) (or get new ones). Try to get a piece the same length as the old housing. But if it needs shortening, use a knife to peel off the outer skin and metal cutters to cut the inner coil. File or trim off any sharp metal burrs that may damage the wire. The housing that runs to the rear wheel is usually attached to the frame by small clips. If the clips have small screws, just loosen them to replace the housing. On many lightweights, the housing is in two pieces and fits into loops on the frame. Replace it the way it was originally.

Hand Brake Troubles

Problem	What to check for
One brake shoe drags.	Rim unit not centered.
	Pivotal bolt on side-pull unit is loose.
	Rim unit needs oil on pivotal bolt(s).
	Spring in rim unit bent or broken.*
	One pivotal bolt on center-pull unit is too tight.
Brakes slip (or brake too slowly).	Brake shoes not close enough to rim (stretched cable).
	Worn brake shoes.
	Oil on rim or brake shoes.
Brakes jam or drag (won't release rim).	Pivotal bolt(s) need oiling.
	Pivotal bolt(s) too tight.
	Hand lever too tight or bent.
	Cable wire frayed, getting caught in housing.
	Brake arms bent.*
	Spring in rim unit broken.*
Cable breaks frequently.	Cable wire is wearing on damaged or poorly cut housing.
Brakes squeal.	Rubber has burnt onto the rim; clean off with solvent.
	Old brake shoes; rubber has hardened.
	Grit on brake shoes.
Uneven braking, usually with "shuttering."	Rim unit is loose.
	Wheel warped (see p. 136).
	Rim of wheel is bent.*

* Difficult to repair; best to go to a bike shop.

Coaster Brakes

Most people who have ever ridden a bike are familiar with coaster brakes. They are the brakes that are activated by back pedaling and which for many years were a characteristic feature of most American-made bikes.

The entire coaster-brake mechanism is inside the hub of the rear wheel. When you back pedal, the rear sprocket turns backwards and screws a large nut—a "clutch"—into the brake causing brake shoes to expand against the inside of the hub and stop the wheel. When you pedal forward, the clutch is screwed into the hub shell and the sprocket turns the wheel. When you just stop pedaling, the clutch disengages and frees the sprocket, and you coast. This is why they are called "coaster" brakes. If the wheel were driven directly by the sprocket, as it was on early bikes and still is on track bikes, the bike could be stopped by back pedaling, but you wouldn't be able to coast unless you pulled up your feet and let the pedals spin, the way a child does on a tricycle.

This process takes longer than it does to apply hand brakes, and this slower reaction time is the major disadvantage of coaster brakes. The other is that they are mechanically complex and hard to get to. But they do have advantages, especially for children, who often don't have the strength to work hand brakes. Since the mechanism is inside the hub, it is protected from rough handling and weather and doesn't need the frequent adjustments that hand brakes do. It is not likely to "go" suddenly, the way that a hand brake does if the cable snaps, or to fail in rainy weather.

Coaster brakes should give years of trouble-free use, but if any serious trouble develops, you should go to a mechanic. The rear hub does need to be oiled—and the nut holding the brake arm needs to be tightened—as a part of routine maintenance (see pp. 92–93).

Chain Drive

Note: For derailleur bikes, turn to p. 46.

The function of the chain drive is to deliver the power that you put on the pedals to the back wheel at an increased ratio so that the wheel drives the bike faster than you pedal (explained on p. 68). This part of your bike is worked harder, gets grimier, and probably receives less attention than any other part. It consists of the crank, two sprockets, and the chain.

Only the chain is likely to give you any trouble. The steel sprockets on non-derailleur bikes are not easily removed and are durable enough so that they rarely need more attention than cleaning. The same is true of most cranks, and the only time you are likely to work on a crank is when you adjust or overhaul the bearings in the crank housing. The procedure for these is described on pp. 97–99. You should note that the crank on American-made bikes is one piece of bent steel from pedal to pedal, with the front sprocket attached—usually permanently. On imported bikes, the crank has three pieces: a left crank arm, a right crank arm with the front sprocket attached, and an axle running through the frame.

The chain on non-derailleur bikes is usually ⅛-inch wide and is held together by a removable link called the "master link." Chains usually break at the master link and can be fixed by replacing the master link. A spare one can be bought at any bike store. A chain needs to be cleaned and oiled regularly (see p. 93) and replaced when worn—usually every couple of years. The best test for a worn chain is to grab the top and bottom of the chain just behind the front sprocket and pull it tightly around the sprocket. If you can lift the chain off the sprocket more than ½-inch, replace it. The tension on a chain should be adjusted so that it has about ½-inch play up and down. Noise is a sign of chain trouble. A worn chain rattles. A tight link causes a steady kerplunking sound.

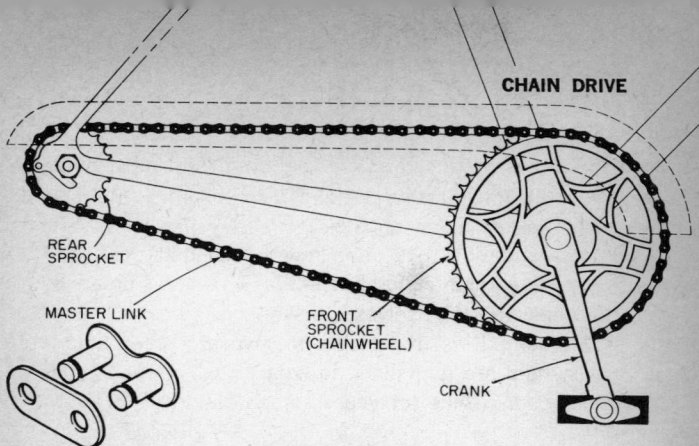

CHAIN DRIVE

REAR SPROCKET

MASTER LINK

FRONT SPROCKET (CHAINWHEEL)

CRANK

Note: To work on the chain, put your bike upside down, on a rack or on its left (non-chain) side, resting on cardboard.

To remove chain: Find master link and pry off the oversize plate (or clip holding removable plate on). The rest of the master link will slide out.

To replace chain: Get chain on rear sprocket before you insert master link and snap plate back on. Then, put on like a thrown chain (see below). A new chain should be same length and width as the old one.

To get a thrown chain back on: Reseat chain on rear sprocket. Then, put a couple of links on front sprocket and, while holding them on, turn the pedals, and the chain will seat itself. If you have trouble, loosen the rear axle nuts and move wheel forward just enough to get chain on.*

To tighten a sagging chain: Loosen the rear axle nuts and pull wheel back until chain has no more than 1/2-inch play.*

To fix a tight link: Watch the chain as it goes over the rear sprocket. A tight link will jump. Put some light oil on the link and work it loose by gently flexing it from side to side.

To remove chain guard: Chain guards are held onto the frame by two or three clips with screws. Find these and it's easy to remove and replace the chain guard.

To remove crank and front sprocket: See pp. 97–99. Rear sprockets are best left to a mechanic.

* Refer to p. 135 for gear and brake disconnections.

Children's Bikes

Most bikes produced are for children. And most parents who walk into a store looking for a bike for their child encounter an array of bikes that they find bewildering. In this situation they often buy a bike that they believe will please their child, but actually may be doing both the child and themselves a disservice.

Although it is impossible to give any hard and fast rules, here are guidelines to keep in mind when you are looking for a bike for your preteen child:

Bike size is very important. It may be economical to buy clothing a size too large for your child, but with a bike it's. different. On most children's bikes, the handlebars and seats can be adjusted upward enough to allow for two or three years growth. But when you first get a bike, your child should be able to get on and off easily when the seat is all the way down. And on boy's models, your child should be able to straddle the frame comfortably with both feet on the ground. On your child's first bike, size is critical. A child perched on a large bike, barely able to reach the pedals, will be so afraid of falling off that he'll never be able to learn to ride. On later bikes, it's a matter of safety. Children, through daring or lack of judgment, often find themselves in situations that adults would avoid in the first place.

On children's bikes, the size is determined by the diameter of the wheel, and the most common wheel sizes are 12, 16, 20, and 24 inches. Most children can't safely ride a bike unless their leg length (inseam) is two or three inches longer than the wheel size on a bike with a conventional seat; more if the bike has a banana seat. Full-size bikes with 26-inch wheels and a small frame size (short seat tube) can be ridden by many preteenagers. The smallest frame size made is around 17 inches. (For more on frame size, see p. 7).

Gears are an expensive luxury on children's bikes. On most single-speeds, the combination of chain sprockets and small wheel size gives them a relatively low gear ratio. Although this ratio doesn't let the child go very fast, it makes the bike easy to pedal over all but very steep hills. If your older child needs gears for long rides or steep hills, 3-speed hub gears should be adequate.

Brakes that are operated by back pedaling—"coaster brakes"—are better for children than hand brakes. Coaster brakes, which are inside the hub of the rear wheel, are protected from weather and abuse and require little attention. Hand brakes, which are exposed, require frequent adjustment and will fail if the rims of the wheel are wet, if a cable snaps, or if the brake unit is knocked askew. In addition, many young children do not have hands large enough or strong enough to operate hand levers. However, bikes with hub gears should have hand brakes; coaster brakes are not reliable when they are combined with gears in the rear hub.

Accessories should be kept to a minimum, especially if your child is learning to ride. They only distract a child who should be concentrating on riding. A bell is okay, but make sure your child knows to stop for pedestrians and not to expect them to move when they hear his bell. If your older child rides at night, front and rear lights are necessary. And day or night, the more reflectors a child's bike has, the better. Training wheels should be removed if you want your child to learn to balance and ride. Even when they are raised an inch or so, a child tends to lean to one side and ride his bike like a tricycle.

On the next page the types of children's bikes are described. Teaching your child to ride is covered on p. 76. Teenagers can ride adult bikes (see pp. 6–15).

Types

Sidewalk bikes are inexpensive toy-quality bikes, but they are suitable for children under six. At this age they are only going to ride up and down the sidewalk or driveway or around the playground, and they don't need a good quality, expensive bike. Most of these bikes are also called "convertibles" because the top tube can be removed or lowered to change the bike from a boy's model to a girl's. But it's much easier for a beginner to learn to ride if the tube is removed or lowered. Most of these bikes have hard rubber tires and few bearings, and often one won't last more than the couple of years that your child will use it. If you want to pass a bike on to another child, you may want to get a better quality middleweight. Many sidewalk bikes come without brakes; be sure to get one with a coaster brake. Also be sure to get rubber-treaded pedals, not the slippery plastic ones. You probably will need a bike with 16-inch wheels for your four-to six-year-old. Bikes with 12- and 20-inch wheels are also available.

Middleweights were the standard American children's bike until the mid-1960's, when the high-rise bike was introduced. And they are still the best bikes for children from six to eleven. They have a heavy but durable frame with curved tubes, the boy's models having the distinctive rounded "camelback" shape (see frame shapes, p. 44). They have coaster brakes, no gears, and wide, low-pressure "balloon" tires that give a stable, cushioned ride. One with 20-inch wheels can be ridden by most children from six until nine and one with 24-inch wheels from eight until eleven. One with 26-inch wheels usually has a very small frame size and can be ridden from ten on. Middleweights are also made with 16-inch wheels for younger children. Prices vary, but none are very expensive.

High-rise bikes are very popular bicycles for children today, but their faddish motorcycle styling and the questions that have been raised about their safety seem to indicate that their popularity may be short-lived. These bikes vary greatly in special features and in price. But all of them have high-rise handlebars and long banana seats. And nearly all of them have the same heavy, sturdy frame as the middleweight, although the frame and the wheels are smaller, relative to the rider, because of the higher handlebars and seat. The less expensive ones have coaster brakes and no gears. In the middle price range, they usually have hand brakes and 3-speed hub gears. And expensive ones, which only come in boy's models, have hand brakes, 5-speed derailleur gears, and special features such as smaller front wheels, extra wide back wheels, and suspension springs.

High risers are known for their maneuverability, and most children find them fun to ride and show off on. But their safety has been questioned by the Children's Hazards Division of the Food and Drug Administration and by many others. Common objections are: The higher seat and smaller wheels make the bike unstable, especially when the front wheel is smaller than the back; the high-rise handlebars, which are gripped spread-eagle, make the bike harder to steer; and the banana seat encourages children to ride together, the cause of many accidents.

Racing-style derailleur bikes with 24-inch wheels or 26-inch wheels and a small frame are replacing high risers in popularity and are much safer; but the gears are more than most preteenagers can handle. In quality, they belong to the lowest category of derailleurs (see p. 10).

English 3-speed bikes with 24-inch wheels or 26-inch wheels and a small frame are best if your child needs gears (see p. 8).

City Riding

In urban areas, where the distances you usually travel are never great but are rarely so short that you can walk them quickly, an almost ideal way to get around is on a bicycle. In the slow moving traffic in the center of a city, it is as fast as a car—faster if you consider that you will usually have no trouble finding a parking space at your destination. If you use a bike for commuting and you live under five miles from work, you can be home within a half hour, riding at a leisurely pace. As several experiments by cycling commuters have shown, door to door, in most cities, a bike is faster than any other mode of transportation. And, of course, a bike is healthful, non-polluting, and cheap.

Bicycles would be truly ideal if everyone rode them. But unfortunately, the streets that bikes are used on are usually clogged with vehicles fifty to a hundred times heavier, making it the exposed cyclist and not the enclosed motorist whose skin is at stake. Some cities have set aside bike lanes, and hopefully, more will as the numbers of cyclists increase. But in the meantime, most city cyclists must contend with cars. However, if you ride alertly and cautiously—and never too fast—cycling in the city can be almost as safe as riding anywhere else.

Some suggestions for making riding in the city safer are given on the following pages. But other chapters are also of special interest to city cyclists. Since the theft of bikes is most prevalent in cities, you should read "Locking and parking" on pp. 80–81. From the descriptions of the types of bikes on pp. 6–15, you should be able to choose one that is suitable for the kind of city riding you do. The best seat height for riding in traffic is discussed on p. 112. Clothing suggestions which will make commuting more pleasant in unpredictable weather are given on pp. 40–41 along with safety wear. And, finally, for getting your bike out of the city, see p. 130.

Suggested Rules

Ride with the flow of traffic. This is required by law in most areas, and it is a good safety precaution. In head-on collisions, a cyclist doesn't stand a chance. But if two objects moving in the same direction collide, the impact will be lessened.

Ride along the side of the street, not out in the traffic lanes. No matter how fast you are going—and it's not safe to go very fast in city traffic—cars will need to pass you, and it's safest for you if they do it when you are on the side of the street. If you are riding with the flow of traffic, you will be riding on the right side of the street—except on one-way streets.

Avoid main thoroughfares as much as possible, even if it means going a few blocks out of your way. Both high-speed roadways and traffic-clogged main streets are dangerous for cyclists, and you can usually find quieter parallel streets that will take you where you want to go. These side streets are not only safer but more pleasant and healthier than riding in a stream of exhaust fumes. If you ride to work, plan a route that circumvents as much heavy or fast traffic as possible. Don't overlook using parks, alleys, and winding residential streets.

Watch out at intersections. Most bike accidents occur at intersections. If you have a red light, stop. Don't make a right turn against the light just because it's easy to do on a bike. If a light is changing, don't try to beat it. At a stop-sign-controlled intersection, it's best to stop, even if you have the right of way, and make sure that cars coming from the other direction have stopped completely and are aware of you before you cross. Whenever you stop, it's a good idea to pull up as far as you can, almost into the pedestrian crossing so that the driver of the lead car behind you can see you. Use hand signals, too, if you plan to turn or stop. Use caution—even if you have a green light and are going straight ahead, watch out for cars turning in front of you.

Don't make left turns. Getting from the right side of one street to the right side of a crossing street in one turn requires you to cut through two lanes of traffic—the on-going cars next to you and the on-coming cars in front of you—and this is not very safe. To avoid this, it's best to go straight across the street you are on, stop, turn your bike, wait for the light to change, and then go across with the light. Of course, if there is little or no traffic, you can carefully pull into the center traffic lane as you approach the corner, signal your turn, and, when you are sure on-coming cars have passed or stopped, you can turn.

Watch parked cars. Since you'll usually be riding next to a row of them, you have to be careful that a door doesn't suddenly open in front of you. You also have to be careful of parked or waiting cars that might suddenly pull out in your path. Glance at the line of parked cars ahead of you. If someone is in a car, if the brake lights are on, if exhaust is coming out of the tail pipe, slow down and make sure the car is not about to pull out. And if the cars approaching from behind permit, veer far enough out to avoid an opening door.

Watch driveways for cars or trucks that are backing out. Anytime you see garages, filling stations, parking lots, or loading platforms ahead of you, slow down and look.

Don't ride near buses. The driver usually can't see you, and he may at any moment suddenly pull into the curb to make a stop. If you have to pass a stopped bus on the left, give it as wide a berth as you can. But first, see how many people are getting on the bus. If only one or two people are getting on, don't try to pass it. You may have to tag along behind a bus for several blocks before you can pass it. Be sure to stay a good distance behind it. If you are riding on a one-way street with buses, ride on the left side of the street and avoid their lane entirely.

Watch taxis and delivery trucks. They often stop suddenly in the middle of the block and pull into the curb.

Look for pedestrians. They're not looking for cyclists, and often, if they don't see a car coming, they'll cross right in front of you, sometimes darting out from between parked cars. Of course, whenever pedestrians have the right of way, you should give it to them. And, in the middle of the city, remember that the sidewalks are for them, not cyclists.

Slow down or stop for double-parked vehicles until the traffic permits you to pull into the traffic lane to pass. Make sure the vehicle is not about to pull out. Double-parked trucks are a serious hazard since you usually can't see past them.

Watch the road surface, as always, but be careful not to swerve into traffic to avoid a pothole. If you can't slow down or stop and let the traffic go by, hold tight, stand up, and ride straight over the hole. Don't try to hit it at an angle, for you can catch your wheel and fall. In the city, gratings, especially sewer gratings, are another problem.

Avoid rush hours if you can, especially the evening rush hour when most bike accidents occur. If you are commuting you can't avoid the traffic, but if you are riding for pleasure you can plan to ride when the streets are not so crowded.

Clothing

For ordinary cycling—especially long rides—clothing that is lightweight, not bulky, and fairly close fitting will save weight, allow freer movement, and give less wind resistance. But clothing that is too tight can restrict movement and circulation. Colors that are light and bright make you more visible to motorists.

If you ride a lot in changeable weather, a lightweight, bright-colored nylon windbreaker is very useful.

Shoes for cycling should be low cut to permit ankle movement, flexible to allow the foot to move freely, and light to save weight. And if they have rubber soles with treads, they will give a better grip. In general, boots, heavy leather shoes, and high heels are not recommended; casual shoes and tennis shoes are. But if you have metal rattrap pedals with sharp teeth, you can feel them through tennis shoes with thin soles. Professional cycling shoes are made, but because they are useful only for riding, they are not practical for most cyclists.

In cold weather, less clothing is needed than you might think because you are warmed up by riding. Actually, wind and humidity may be more important considerations than temperature. Several layers of clothing are better than one heavy coat which may become too hot. A combination such as a zip-up jacket or windbreaker, a sweater or sweatshirt, a shirt and a thermal undershirt will let you remove layers before you become overheated and add more before you become chilled. Your legs are not likely to become cold unless you stop, so heavy pants or jeans are sufficient—supplemented with tights or long johns on very cold days. But your hands are likely to get very cold, and lined mittens with elastic cuffs will keep them warmer than gloves. Ear protection may also be necessary—but be sure you can hear cars. If your feet tend to get cold, try a pair of low-cut lined flexible boots.

Rainwear should be lightweight and compact when folded so that you can carry it with you in unpredictable weather, and it should be light and bright in color so that you can be seen on dull rainy days. Although hard to obtain in this country, the best choice is a cyclist's rain cape, which is similar to a poncho but is designed to fit over the pyramid formed by your trunk and arms when you are riding and comes down far enough to cover your hands and the handlebars. Ponchos tend to flap about in the wind too much. Light vinyl raincoats, which are less specialized, are preferred by many riders, but with one, your pants will be soaked from the knees down. To protect your legs you can wear a rain suit, but most are bulky and poorly ventilated. If you give up on keeping your legs dry, just wear old pants and take a waterproof windbreaker with a hood for rain or cold.

Safety wear should be considered by anyone who rides at night or in heavy traffic. Reflective vests and belts, which can be obtained in sporting goods or safety supply stores, greatly increase your visibility at night; and if the color is fluorescent, in the daytime, too. The belts are very compact. But if you have a jacket or windbreaker just for cycling, you can put some reflective tape on it. Motorcycle crash helmets are a good—but expensive and heavy—safety precaution if you ride in traffic or very fast. Other lighter weight, less protective, and less expensive safety headwear designed for athletes or workmen can be worn, including the leather mesh helmets worn by racing cyclists. Some of the protective headwear sold for workmen look like caps.

Pant clips are a good precaution if you wear loose trousers or bell bottoms, or if your bike doesn't have a chainguard. And, any glasses you wear while riding should have lenses of safety glass or plastic.

Frames

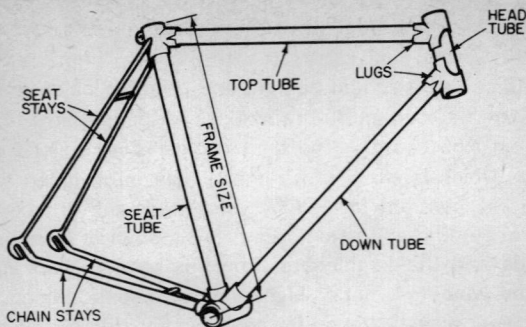

How the frame is made is the major factor in the weight, strength, and cost of a bike. On inexpensive bikes, the tubes in the frame are made from flat steel that has been rounded and welded together, and if you look closely, you can see the seam. For strength, a thick gauge of steel has to be used, and the result is a bike that is heavy and inflexible but usually durable and cheap. On medium-quality bikes, tubes are machine-forged from solid steel and are seamless. Better quality steel is used and the tubing is thinner and the bike lighter but still strong.

As bikes move up in quality, steel alloys with higher tensile strengths are used, and the seamless tubing becomes much thinner. The result is a bike that is light and strong but expensive. The frame will have a springy quality that makes it more responsive when you ride it. The two steel alloys that are commonly used on better frames are chrome-molybdenum steel alloy and manganese-molybdenum alloy. The manganese alloy is the stronger, and tubes made from it are the thinnest.

Although you can't see it, on the best quality lightweights, one, some, or all of the seamless manganese alloy tubes are thicker at the ends in order to withstand the greater stress on the angles of the frame. Seamless tubes of this kind are called "double-butted." The brand names Reynolds 531 and Columbus on manganese steel tubing are respected signs of quality——especially when the tubes are double-butted——but other good seamless tubing is available.

Because of the stress on the joints, the way the tubes are joined is important, too. On inexpensive bikes the seamed tubes are welded together at very high temperatures and, since the tubes are thick, this process is adequate. But if high-temperature welding is used on thinner tubing, it weakens the metal at these stress points. On better bikes, the tubes are fitted into a sleeve at the joint, called a "lug" and the tubes are welded into the lugs at lower temperatures——a process advertised as "brazing." A lugged and brazed frame usually indicates good quality. Some better bikes, however, do have brazed lugless frames, but they use extra-thick brazing.

The finish on frames also varies with their quality, but any adult bike should have a hard baked-enamel finish.

Repairs: Most frames are quite durable and won't fail with average riding unless they have a manufacturing defect——which should show up in the first few hundred miles of riding. But if a frame is bent or broken and you have it straightened or rewelded, the metal in that part of the frame will be dangerously weak. The only safe thing is to buy a new bike——one with a stronger frame that can take the rough handling you give it.

Repainting a frame is useless. Even enamel chips.

Frame size: The measurement that is used to describe the size of a frame is the length of the seat tube from the point where the seat post enters it, to the center of the bottom bracket. On adult bikes, this varies from 17 to 26 inches. The other tubes are proportionally longer or shorter. Getting a bike with the right frame size for you is very important (see p. 7).

Frame Shapes

A diamond frame is used on all full-sized men's bicycles. The two triangles that form it are structurally a very strong design, as has been proved by its many years of use by racers.

An open frame is used on nearly all women's and girl's bikes, and in a modified form on all folding bikes and adult tricycles. On most women's bikes the tubes are straight (upper illustration). But on girl's middleweights the tubes are curved (lower illustration). On most folding bikes there is only one heavy down tube. Although an open frame is not as structurally strong as the frames used on men's bikes, it is fine for most riding. But for touring and hard riding, a diamond frame is better.

A camelback cantilevered frame is used on boy's middleweight and high-rise bikes. The design is structurally strong, but this frame is usually made of heavy welded and unlugged tubes.

A mixte frame is used on some better quality women's lightweights. Like the open frame, it can be ridden with a skirt, but it is stronger and more stable because of the twin diagonal tubes. ("Mixte" means "mixed" in French.)

Other unusual shapes are used, especially on high-rise bikes, usually to disguise a heavy welded frame.

Forks

The fork is usually made of the same material as the frame and is of comparable quality. On inexpensive bikes, the blades and crown of the fork are made from a solid piece of metal, and the fork is strong, inflexible, and heavy. Better bikes have forks with tubular blades brazed into the crown, and they are lighter and absorb bumps better.

The fork, the stem, and the handlebars form the steering column of a bike. The tube at the top of the fork fits into the head tube of the frame and the handlebar stem is wedged into the fork tube. The fork tube rotates on ball bearings inside the head tube of the frame. These bearings periodically need to be removed and regreased, and they can be adjusted if you have steering difficulties (see pp. 95–98).

The only serious problem you are likely to have with a fork is bending it —usually by running into something head on. If you do bend one, it's safest and not too expensive to replace it. The procedure for replacing it is the same as for overhauling the headset (p. 98).

Another difference in forks is in the angle of the bend of the fork arms— which is called the "rake." On most bikes, this angle is fairly wide and gives a springy ride; but some better bikes have a smaller rake, preferred by racers because it holds the road better.

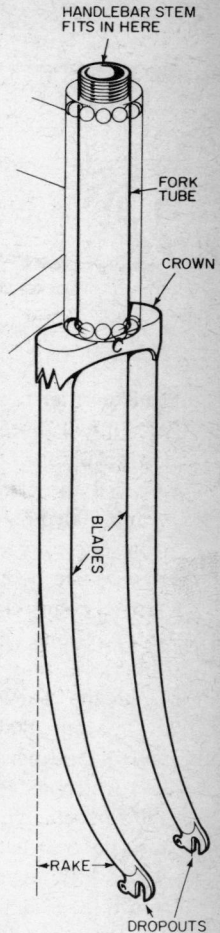

HANDLEBAR STEM FITS IN HERE

FORK TUBE

CROWN

BLADES

RAKE

DROPOUTS

Derailleur Gears

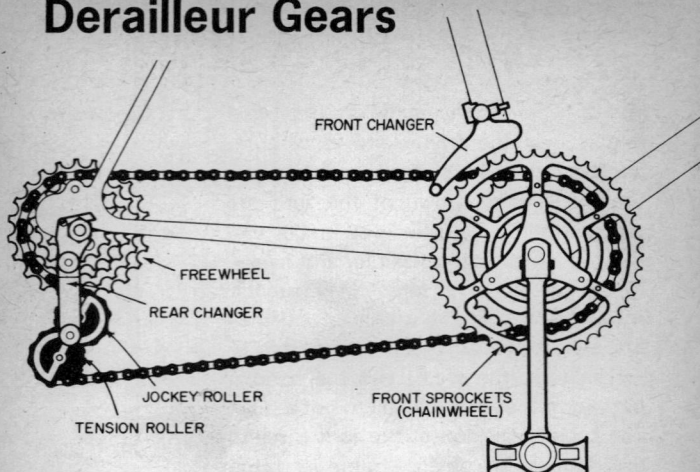

Unlike other bikes, derailleur bikes have multiple sprockets (metal discs with teeth that the chain goes around). On a 10-speed, the most common derailleur bike, there are five sprockets on the rear wheel and two on the pedal crank. As you shift the gears, the chain jumps ("derails") from one sprocket to another. And as it does, the effort required to pedal and the distance you travel each pedal turn changes. It is easy to see how these gears work if you put your bike upside down and shift the gears while you are turning the pedals.

On the rear of most derailleur bikes there is a cluster of five sprockets, and because it lets you coast, it is called the freewheel. There is also an elongated mechanism which moves the chain along the freewheel. This is the rear changer or rear derailleur. It is the most important part of the system and the most complex—because it has to both move the chain from sprocket to sprocket and to keep it tight. The part of the changer that carries the chain is the cage, which has two rollers that the chain loops around in a backward S. The lower roller keeps tension on the chain and is called the tension roller, and the upper roller "jockeys" the chain from sprocket to sprocket and is called the jockey roller. The body of the changer is a parallelogram-shaped device which moves the cage in and out and at the same time keeps it vertically aligned with the sprockets. As you pull the gear lever back, this device pushes the cage in, towards the bike, moving the chain to a larger sprocket. As you push the lever up, the cage springs out, moving the chain to a smaller sprocket. At the points where the cage and the body are joined and where the body is attached to the mounting plate, the derailleur is pivoted, which allows it to swing forward as more chain is needed on larger sprockets and to spring back and reel in chain as less is needed on smaller sprockets.

On a 5-speed bike, this is all you will have. In the lowest gear, the chain is on the largest (inside) sprocket of the freewheel. It is much lower than the low gear on a 3-speed and makes it easy to climb hills. In the highest gear, the chain is on the smallest (outer) sprocket. This gear is the equivalent of the high gear on a 3-speed. The other three gears are in-between.

On a 10- or 15-speed bike, you'll also find a multiple front sprocket, another gear lever, and a front changer. Since it doesn't keep tension on the chain and only makes one or two shifts, this changer is uncomplicated, consisting of a simple chain guide moved by a smaller parallelogram shifter or spring-controlled rod.

With two front sprockets, a total of ten gear combinations are possible with the five rear sprockets. With three, fifteen are possible. In the lowest gear, the chain is on the smallest front sprocket and the largest rear sprocket and the chain is all the way in towards the bike. In the highest gear, the chain is on the largest front and the smallest rear sprocket and is all the way out. But exactly what the gear ratios are will depend on how much variation there is in the size of the sprockets (in the number of teeth they have). On most common 10-speeds, there is a large variation in the size of the sprockets and these bikes have a wide range of gears—including a good selection of low gears—which give the rider a gear for every condition—hills, wind, load, and road surface. But some better 10-speeds that are used for racing have only a close range of high gears. The gear range of any derailleur can be changed by simply replacing sprockets—usually the freewheel. But the capacity of some derailleurs is limited, so check the capacity of yours first. Also, figure out what gears you will be getting. If a sprocket change is not thought out, you may get repeated gear ratios. Gear ratios are explained on p. 68, and a table for figuring them out is given there.

On a 15-speed, the third front sprocket is usually a small one—to give extra low gears for mountainous terrain. But since extreme sprocket combinations strain the system, not all 15 gears can be used effectively.

Except for some of the ones used on cheap 10-speeds, most derailleurs are of good quality. Like other lightweight components, weight is a major factor in price, but since it is measured in ounces, most riders can ignore it. Here are some good commonly found brands:

Campagnolo: The "Record" and "Nuovo Record" models are the lightest and best derailleurs made, but expensive. The "Valentino" is somewhat lower in quality. The pole-type front changer is good but hard to adjust.

Huret "Allvit" ("Sprint"): Good derailleur made of stamped steel, but will become sluggish if not kept clean.

Simplex "Prestige": Good, but made with a lot of Delrin, a plastic which gives it a smooth operation, but a short life if abused. The pole-type front changer is hard to adjust.

Shimano: Very good, sturdy, and inexpensive, but heavy.

Sun Tour: Also very good, sturdy, inexpensive, and heavy.

Using Derailleur Gears

Changing gears on a derailleur bike is a skill, and it takes time to learn to use them effectively. Many people find that it takes a while just to learn to ride a lightweight without wobbling and even longer to ride well enough to feel comfortable leaning over and touching the gear levers. But with practice anyone who can ride a bike can learn to use derailleur gears.

Like most skills, shifting gears on a derailleur is a matter of timing and coordination. It may seem tricky at first, but there are only three things to remember:

Change gears only when you are pedaling forward. If you stop pedaling to change them, you can rack up the chain or chew up the sprockets when you start pedaling again. If you try to change them while you are back pedaling, you can bend the changers.

Relax the pressure on the pedals when you shift. This doesn't mean to slow down but to ease up on the pressure you are putting on the pedals. The changer can't carry the chain onto another sprocket if you are pushing the pedals hard and there is a lot of tension on the chain. If you are going uphill, your bike has to have enough momentum to carry it forward with light pedaling pressure when you shift. Never force a lever.

Make the shift quickly and firmly. This is not easy at first since the levers on most derailleurs don't click into position the way that they do on 3-speeds. You have to learn where the gears are through trial and error. If you shift properly, you should hear only a plunking sound when the chain seats itself on the sprocket. If you hear grinding or chattering, it is not seated correctly, and the lever needs to be adjusted slightly. On a 10-speed, when you move one lever often the other will need adjusting.

When you first ride a derailleur bike, repeatedly practice shifting gears, changing them one at a time in sequence. Remember that as the chain moves out, the
higher the gear will be—and though your bike will be
harder to pedal, it will go a longer distance with each
pedal turn. As the chain moves in, the gear will be lower
—and your bike will be easier to pedal, but will go a
shorter distance with each pedal turn.

On a 5-speed, your gears will be a simple progression
from 1 to 5 as the chain moves out along the freewheel.
But on a 10-speed, you will find that your combinations
are not a simple progression. You can't simply use the
five sprockets of the freewheel with the small front
sprocket and then with the large front sprocket. The
sprocket combinations overlap in the middle gears. The
best thing is to memorize the gear combinations or to
make a list of them and tape it to your handlebars until
you learn them. An example of the gear combinations on
a 10-speed with a wide range of gears is shown on p. 70,
and you can figure out your own gears from the table
there. Keep in mind that extreme sprocket combinations
—when the chain is on the large front and the largest
rear sprockets or the small front and the smallest rear—
place a strain on the derailleur system, and it is good to
avoid them. This is not your highest and lowest gears, but
two of your middle gears, and on most bikes there are
other combinations that are very close to these two, so
you can easily avoid them. Skipping them also makes it
easier to learn the progression of gears.

After you have learned to shift gears, the next step is
to learn to use them effectively. To do this, remember
that the gears are there to help you keep a steady, natural pedaling rhythm. On a lightweight, the least tiring
rhythm is a rapid one of from 60 to 80 pedal turns a
minute. The best way to keep this cadence mile after

mile is to ride with slightly lower gears than you feel you need. The time to shift gears is just before it is necessary to change your pedaling rhythm. It doesn't take too much riding to discover when to make "just before" shifts.

Keeping an eye on the terrain ahead of you will make it possible for you to do this. When you see a hill coming up, judge which low gear or gears will be necessary to get you over it without changing cadence. Don't use your lowest gear to get over every hill. Start shifting just before pedal resistance increases and while you still have enough speed to relax the pressure on the pedals. You may end up walking up a few hills, but you can only learn both when to change gears and what gear to use by experimenting.

The same is true of riding on a level surface. As you develop a natural pedaling rhythm, you'll find that a gear no longer feels right when conditions change—such as road surface or wind. On a rougher road or with a head wind, you'll shift down. You'll also discover which low gear will compensate for a load or fatigue.

If you are a beginner, avoid using the high gears until you are sure that you have good control over your bike. Even then, the high gears should be used only to gain speed when pedal resistance starts to drop. This will occur going downhill, with a strong tail wind, or with a lot of built-up momentum on a flat surface. Riding in high gear just for speed is fun for short sprints, but for longer distances your regular pedaling pace will slow down, and you'll soon be exhausted.

Because derailleurs can only be shifted while you are pedaling and it can be difficult to start up again if you are in a high gear, there is a temptation to run traffic lights and stop signs. But if you look ahead, you can shift down before you have to stop. Safety, not gearing, should be your first consideration.

Derailleur Maintenance

Adjustments and simple repairs for the most common types of derailleur parts are given on the following pages, and following that, on p. 61, there is a trouble-shooting chart for derailleur problems. Any rider should be able to make these adjustments and repairs, but remember derailleurs are complex mechanisms subjected to hard use, and the system as a whole has to be balanced, so you will need patience until you get a feel for making the adjustments on your derailleur.

Here are some things to keep in mind: Before you assume that something is out of adjustment or mechanically wrong with your gears, see if they need cleaning and oiling. Malfunction is often the result of dirty, dry changers or grimy chains. Of course, the best way to avoid these problems is to clean and oil your derailleur regularly (see facing page). The trouble-shooting chart should give you a fairly good idea of what is wrong with your gears; but before you start turning adjusting screws, put your bike upside down and observe the entire gear system closely as you turn the pedals and shift the gears that are giving you trouble. The cause will often be obvious. On a new bike, the most likely cause of difficulty will be stretched cables; it takes several weeks for the cables to stop stretching. The same is true when you replace a cable. On older bikes, worn chains and freewheel sprockets are likely to be a source of trouble. Finally, after adjusting them, test the gears by riding.

Serious problems, such as a badly bent or damaged changer, should be taken to a bike mechanic. With less expensive derailleurs, it is often cheaper to replace a damaged unit than to get it fixed—especially if it is old. The best rule is to price both. And don't avoid replacing your damaged changer with a cheaper one. Some of the Japanese-made ones are of very good quality.

Tools: You will need several small metric wrenches, and most bike stores sell inexpensive sets. For some derailleurs, you may also need metric Allen wrenches or a small Phillips screwdriver. In addition, you should get a chain rivet tool to remove and replace the chain and a freewheel tool to remove the freewheel (see pp. 58–59).

Cleaning and oiling: To function well, the changers and freewheel need to be oiled—and the chain cleaned and oiled—once a month (see p. 91). The levers, which work on friction, should never be oiled. Every few months, the changers and freewheel should be cleaned thoroughly. You can use an old toothbrush to work a solvent, such as kerosene, into the parts. Be careful not to get solvent on the tires. After you have dried the parts, reoil them with a light oil and wipe off the excess. Every six months, the freewheel should be removed, soaked in solvent (to clean out internal grit), dried, and reoiled. This can also be done if a freewheel jams. A changer that is dirty can also be removed and soaked in solvent.

Alignment: Misalignment of the front and rear sprockets is often the cause of shifting difficulty and strange noises that you can't seem to find a cause for. To check the alignment on a 10-speed, sight through the space between the two front sprockets. If the alignment is correct, you should see the middle sprocket of the freewheel. On a 5-speed, the single front sprocket should align with the middle freewheel sprocket. If your bike sprockets are out of alignment, take it to a bike shop. Misaligned sprockets cause a lot of unnecessary wear.

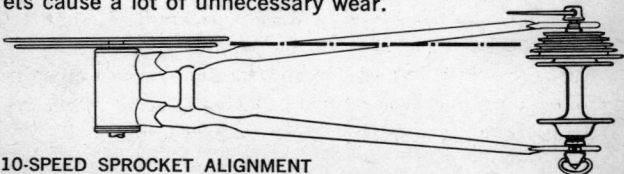

10-SPEED SPROCKET ALIGNMENT

SLOT FOR CABLE

PIVOTAL SCREW

Levers

To adjust lever: Tighten or loosen the pivotal screw until it is just tight enough to allow the lever to move smoothly.

To clean sticking lever: Closely observing the sequence of washers, remove the pivotal screw to disassemble lever. Clean parts with solvent (kerosene) and, if rusty, steel wool. Reassemble the same way.

Cables

To replace a broken or damaged cable: Loosen anchor bolt on changer to release cable. Unscrew pivotal screw on lever and remove leaded end of cable from slot in lever. Pull cable wire out of housing. Get a new cable of the same diameter and same length (or slightly longer) and with the same leaded end. Put changer and chain on smallest sprocket. Mount leaded end of cable in lever and retighten screw. Make sure lever moves freely. Lightly grease cable where it will pass through housing before threading it through. Put cable through anchor bolt, pull snug, but not taut. Check position of lever before retightening anchor bolt. Cut excess cable only after cable is installed. (If housing also needs to be replaced, see p. 27.)

To adjust cable tension on rear changer: Loosen lockring and screw adjusting sleeve in or out as needed. Retighten lockring. If this is not enough, put adjusting sleeve in middle position. Then, while holding cable, loosen anchor bolt, pull (or let out) cable until it is snug but not taut. Retighten. Adjust sleeve.

To adjust cable tension on front changer: While holding cable, loosen anchor bolt and pull (or let out) cable until it is snug but not taut. Retighten anchor bolt.

LOCK RING

ADJUSTING SLEEVE

ANCHOR BOLT

Front Changers

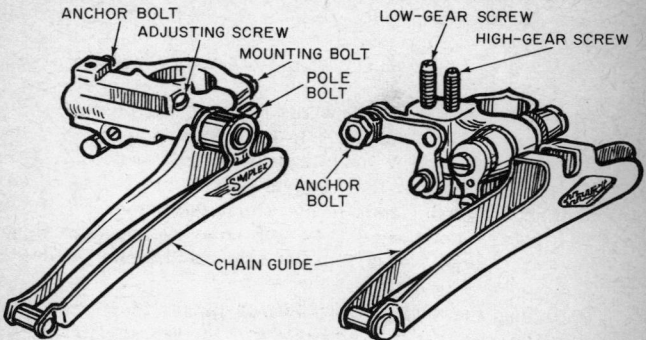

| POLE-TYPE | PARALLELOGRAM-TYPE |

To adjust parallelogram-type (with two adjusting screws): Put bike into its lowest gear (inner sprockets).* Adjust the low-gear screw until the chain just misses touching the inner side of the chain guide. Then, put the bike into its highest gear (outer sprockets)* and adjust the high-gear screw until chain just clears outer edge of chain guide.

To adjust pole-type (with one adjusting screw): Put bike into its lowest gear (inner sprockets).* Loosen the bolt that holds chain guide on the pole and move guide until chain just clears the inner edge of the chain guide. Make sure the guide is parallel with the curve of the large sprocket and carefully retighten. Then, put the bike into its highest gear (outer sprockets)* and move the adjusting screw in or out until chain just clears outer edge of chain guide.

To reposition front changer: Loosen one or both mounting bolts slightly and move changer to correct position—about 1/4 inch above the larger sprocket and parallel with the sprockets when you sight from above. Retighten bolts.

To remove front changer: Remove bolt and roller at end of chain guide. Remove mounting bolts. Reverse to replace.

* Pedals must be turning when you shift gears. Put bike upside down, on a rack, or have someone hold up the back wheel.

Rear Changers

Note: If your derailleur isn't shown here, shift the chain onto the smallest rear sprocket.* Then, find the two small screws with springs and try both. The one that moves the cage is the high-gear screw; the other, the low-gear screw.

To adjust the low-gear (inward) range: Shift the chain onto the largest rear sprocket.* If the chain won't go on the sprocket, first check that the cable is not loose, and then, if necessary, loosen the low-gear screw until the chain will shift. If the chain tends to overshoot the sprocket (go into the spokes), get the chain on the sprocket and tighten the low-gear screw until its tip just touches the changer body.

To adjust the high-gear (outward) range: Shift the chain onto the smallest rear sprocket.* If the chain won't go on the sprocket, loosen the high-gear screw until the chain will shift. If it still won't, check that the cable is not too tight. If the chain tends to overshoot the sprocket (go into the stays), get the chain on the sprocket and tighten the high-gear screw until its tip just touches the changer body.

* Pedals must be turning when you shift gears. Put bike upside down, on a rack, or have someone hold up the back wheel.

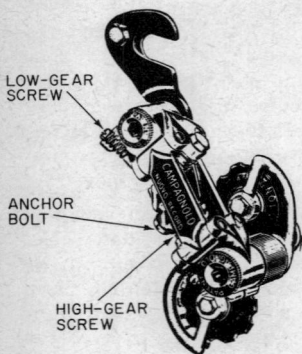

LOW-GEAR SCREW

ANCHOR BOLT

HIGH-GEAR SCREW

CAMPAGNOLO

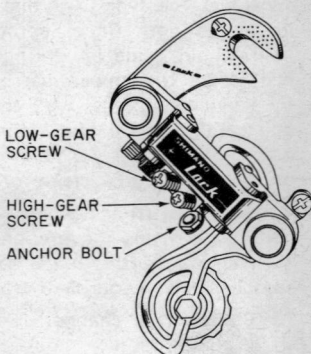

LOW-GEAR SCREW

HIGH-GEAR SCREW

ANCHOR BOLT

SHIMANO

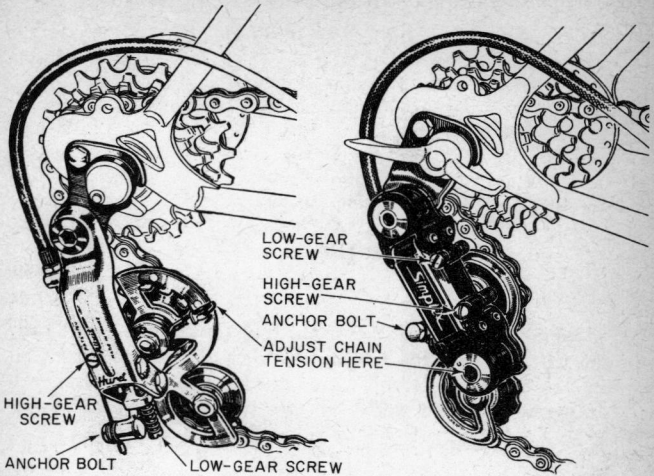

HURET "ALLVIT" ("SPRINT")   SIMPLEX "PRESTIGE"

To adjust chain tension: On Allvit and similar models, move tension spring up a notch to increase tension, down a notch to decrease tension. On Simplex, put an Allen wrench in end of pivotal bolt between changer body and cage (remove dust cap if necessary) and turn clockwise to increase tension and counterclockwise to decrease. Other models should be adjusted by a mechanic. (Also see p. 59).

To remove changer: Shift chain onto smallest sprocket.* Loosen anchor bolt to detach cable. Then, except on Suntour, remove lower (tension) roller by taking out its bolt (to free chain). Remove mounting bolt and loosen axle nut, and the changer will come off. When you replace, reverse procedure, adjusting cable (p. 54) and then gear range.

To check alignment of changer: Shift chain onto smallest sprocket* and with a ruler, check that the two small rollers are aligned perfectly with the sprocket, not tending in or out. Repeat with the largest sprocket. If cage pulls in, the cable may be too tight. But if that is not the cause or if changer is bent, take it to a mechanic or replace it.

Freewheels

To remove freewheel: A special tool is required to fit over the axle and into the freewheel. One type is fluted to fit on splines in the freewheel. The other type (shown) has two prongs to fit into a slot on the freewheel. Get the right one.

1 Remove back wheel (see p. 135), and take off right axle nut (or right nut on quick-release hub; be careful to catch spring). If there is a spacer nut, remove it, too.
2 Insert freewheel tool into freewheel and replace axle nut (or quick-release nut without spring) loosely.
3 Use a wrench and turn the freewheel tool counterclockwise to loosen freewheel. (If too tight, go to a bike shop.)
4 Remove the axle nut and the freewheel tool, and spin the freewheel off by hand. To clean freewheel see p. 53.

To replace freewheel: Carefully screw the freewheel on and tighten by hand. Riding will tighten it the rest of the way. Replace spacer nut and remount wheel.

Note: Don't take a freewheel apart; it's complex. If you replace a freewheel, replace the chain too. Old chains act up on new freewheels. If you replace a freewheel with one that has a new range of gears, make sure your changer can handle the range. And get a longer or shorter chain.

Front Sprockets

To remove on 10- or 15-speed bikes: Remove the bolts (see p. 46) that hold the sprockets onto the fingers of the right crank arm. (For 5-speeds, see pp. 98–99.)

To fix bent tooth: Tighten a crescent wrench on it and bend it straight. Be careful, alloy sprockets are easily bent.

Chains

Note: The chain on a derailleur bike is thinner than the chain on other bikes ($\frac{3}{32}$ inch wide) and doesn't have a master link since it would catch in the rear changer. To remove, or repair a chain you need a chain rivet tool.

To remove chain: Place any link on the chain rivet tool and drive the rivet partly out. When the rivet is almost out, gently flex the chain and it will come apart.

To replace chain: Put the chain on the sprockets with the driven-out rivet toward you. Rejoin the plates, and with the chain-rivet tool, drive the rivet back in until about the same amount of rivet is showing on both sides of the link. Flex the link to make sure it isn't too tight.

To fix tight link: First, put some oil on it and try flexing it to get it loose. If that doesn't work, put the link on the slot nearest the driving point of the chain rivet tool and tighten the point against rivet slightly. If the link is damaged, it can be replaced by using the chain rivet tool to drive its rivets out and to drive the rivets of a new link in. Extra links can be bought at better bike stores.

To determine proper chain length: Put chain (new or old) on the largest rear and the largest front sprockets. If you have a wide range of gears as on most bikes, allow two extra links to get you out of this gear easily. If you have a close range, allow four links. The chain can be shortened or lengthened with the chain rivet tool. Minor adjustments of chain tension can often be done on the rear changer (see p. 57).

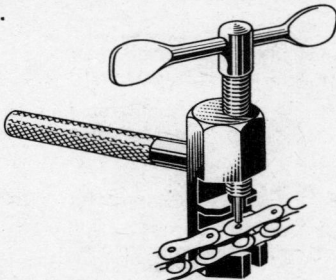

DRIVING RIVET OUT

Derailleur Troubles

Problem	What to check for
Gears change by themselves.	Gear shift lever is loose.
Gears hard to change.	Gear shift lever is tight.
	Cable is too tight.
Gears don't shift all the way or "pause" before shifting; or chain gets caught between sprockets.	Rear changer not vertically aligned.
	Rear changer needs oiling.
	Cable frayed or kinked.
Chain won't go onto smallest rear sprocket (into high gear).	High-gear adjustment screw is in too far.
	Cable is too tight.
Chain comes off largest rear sprocket (into spokes).	Low-gear adjustment screw on rear changer is loose.
Chain won't go onto largest rear sprocket (into low gear).	Low-gear adjustment screw is in too far.
	Cable loose or stretched.
Chain comes off smallest rear sprocket (into spokes).	High-gear adjustment screw on rear changer is loose.
Chain skips, especially on smaller sprockets.	Chain loose; adjust tension on rear changer.
	Chain too long, worn, or has tight link.
	Cable loose or stretched.
	Changer not vertically aligned or is bent.
Chain skips on one sprocket.	Worn sprocket or bent sprocket tooth.

Problem	What to check for
Chain won't stay on (either) front sprocket.	Rear changer not vertically aligned; or is bent.*
	Front changer bent.*
	Chain too long or worn.
	Front changer needs to be repositioned on seat tube.
	Front and rear sprockets not in alignment.*
Chain won't stay on smallest front sprocket.	Low-gear range on front changer needs adjusting.
	Bent or wavy sprocket.*
	Front and rear sprockets not in alignment.*
Chain won't stay on largest front sprocket.	High-gear range of front changer needs adjusting.
	Bent or wavy sprocket.*
	Cable stretched or loose.
Chain rubs against front changer.	Gear range on front changer needs adjustment.
	Front changer needs to be repositioned; or is bent.*
	Bent or wavy front sprocket.*
Noisy rear changer.	Rear changer needs oiling.
	Rear changer not vertically aligned; or is bent.*
Wheel won't move but freewheel does.	Prong in freewheel jammed; clean freewheel.
	Prong in freewheel broken.*

* These repairs are difficult and best handled by a mechanic.

Hub (3-speed) Gears

Hubchanger gears are most commonly found on 3-speed bikes, although 2-, 4-, and 5-speeds are also made. They are called hubchanger gears—or more simply, hub gears—because the gears are located in the hub of the rear wheel. The rear wheel is turned by the rear sprocket—the metal disk with teeth that the chain passes over. These gears work by changing the number of times the wheel turns for every time the sprocket turns.

On a typical 3-speed, the gears are controlled by a trigger unit or twist grip on the handlebars, which is connected by a cable to the gears in the hub. When the rider clicks the control unit, a set of "planet" gears revolving around a "sun" gear on the axle shifts. This causes the wheel to go slower or faster than the rear sprocket—or to turn with it. In normal gear (N or 2), the sprocket and the wheel go around together, and they both turn approximately two and a half times for each turn of the pedals. This gear is the equivalent of riding a single-speed bike. In high gear (H or 3), the wheel goes around one-third faster than the sprocket. A fairly fast speed can be obtained in this gear but can't be maintained for any distance on flat ground because of the effort required. In low gear (L or 1), the wheel goes around one-quarter slower than the sprocket. This is enough to make it easy to climb low hills, but not steep or long ones.

Because they are protected inside the rear hub, hub gears are usually reliable and durable and should give years of service without needing a major repair. But if something really goes wrong with them, the hub has to be opened to repair them—by a good bike mechanic.

The operation of the other speeds is similar to the 3-speed, but on the 2-speed, there is only a normal and a low gear and the gears are changed by backpedaling slightly. The 4- and 5-speeds are becoming rare because of the popularity of derailleur gears.

Changing gears on a 3-speed is easy; it's only a matter of clicking the changer. And they can be changed whether you are riding or standing still. But when you are riding, hub gears change best if there is a slight pause in your pedaling when you shift. When you are standing still, it is sometimes necessary to roll the bike slightly to engage the gears. And if you want to shift two gears at once, it is best to shift into one gear, pedal a couple of times, and then shift again. Remember that low gear (L or 1) requires less pedaling effort and takes you a shorter distance each pedal turn and that high gear (H or 3) requires more effort and takes you further. Here are some suggestions:

Before you start riding—or when you have stopped for a light—shift into low gear so you can take off easily. After you get going, shift into normal (N or 2). Use this gear for most riding on level surfaces. But if you have a heavy load, are tired, or are riding into a strong wind or on a rough surface, use low gear. If you look ahead and judge the terrain coming up, you can save yourself a lot of effort. When you see a hill, try to build up speed—within the limits of safety—before you get to it. If you can, switch to high to gain even more speed and back to normal as you start up. Switch to low gear just before you start to lose speed. If it is a low hill, regular pedaling will get you over. But on a steep or long hill you'll slow down—and you may have to stand up and pump to get over it. When you reach the top of a hill, shift back into normal, and just as you start down, shift into high. If your pedals have lost all their resistance, keep trying them, and when you feel some resistance, start pedaling again if, and only if, you want to gain speed. Whether you pedal or coast, you can pedal in high for a short distance after you reach level. But shift back into normal just before more effort is required.

Gear Range

The gear range and approximate speeds for a typical 3-speed bike with 26-inch wheels (and with the commonly found 46-tooth front sprocket and 18-tooth rear) are:

Gear	Gear number	Distance each pedal turn	Pedal turns per minute		
			45 (slow)	60 (average)	75 (fast)
Low (1)	50	13 feet	6½ mph	9 mph	11 mph
Normal (2)	66	17¼	9	12	15
High (3)	88	23	12	16	20

Gear numbers are explained on pp. 68–71. If your 3-speed doesn't fit the description above, you can use the formulas and tables there to find your gears and speed.

Modifying the gear range: If you live in a hilly area or usually ride with a heavy load, you can have the gear range of your 3-speed lowered so it is less tiring to pedal. The easiest and cheapest way is to have a larger rear sprocket installed on the back wheel. The more teeth the rear sprocket has, the lower the gear range will be and the easier the bike will be to pedal. But remember that you will lose some or all of the speed capability of your high gear. If most of your riding is casual and you rarely use your high gear, this won't be a great loss.

If you don't want to lose your high gear and you have Sturmey Archer gears, you can have a two or three sprocket derailleur system installed on the rear wheel. When combined with the 3-speed hub changer, it will give you a total of six or nine gears. This modification is made with a Cyclo-Benelux conversion kit (for your type of hub). It will give you a good range of gears, though not as good as the ones on 10-speeds.

Either of these modifications can be done by most bike shops that specialize in English bikes.

Maintenance

Adjustment: With regular use, all hub gears will occasionally go out of adjustment. Readjusting them usually only takes a couple of minutes. The procedures for adjusting the two most common types of 3-speed gears are given on the following pages. Sometimes, if your cable has stretched, you also may have to adjust the cable tension.

Oiling: Every month put three or four good squirts of light oil or a tablespoon of light motor oil in the oil fitting of the rear hub. Also put a drop of light oil on the selector unit and on the cable wire where it enters the housing. If you have a bell-crank unit, put a drop on the pivotal points. If you have an indicator chain, oil it lightly.

Problems: If you have difficulty shifting gears, can't shift, find your bike shifting by itself, or find your pedal resistance suddenly gone, your hub gears most probably need adjusting or oiling. If that doesn't work and if no external part is obviously broken or damaged, take your bike to a mechanic to have it repaired. Get an estimate. If your bike is very old, it may be cheaper to get a new rear wheel complete with new hub gears.

Replacements: The external parts of 3-speed gears are easy to replace and the procedures are given on the next two pages. If you replace the cable be sure to get an exact replacement—with the same length of wire and housing and the same leaded end. The "universal" cables that have an anchor bolt on the adjusting sleeve so the cable wire can be shortened or lengthened are not recommended. If the control unit breaks, it's easiest and best to replace it with a standard trigger unit. Of course, if you change the type of control unit, you'll have to change the cable, too.

SPRING
PAWN

FERRULE

CABLE
HOUSING

CABLE
CLAMP

ADJUSTING
SLEEVE

LOCKNUT

INDICATOR
CHAIN

TUBULAR NUT

SHOULDER OF ROD
EVEN WITH AXLE END

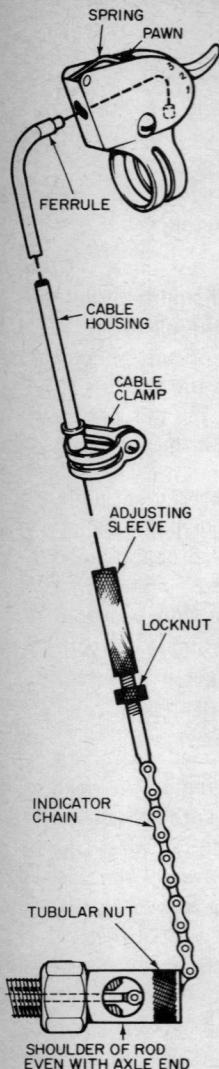

Sturmey-Archer

To adjust: Shift gears to N or 2. Then, loosen locknut and screw adjusting sleeve in or out while looking through the window in the long axle nut. When the shoulder of indicator rod is even with the end of the axle, stop and retighten locknut. Test gears.

To disconnect gears: Loosen locknut and detach cable by unscrewing adjusting sleeve. Then, remove long tubular axle nut and unscrew indicator rod from inside axle.

To reconnect gears: Screw indicator rod into axle snugly but don't force. Replace long axle nut, screw adjusting sleeve onto indicator chain and adjust gears.

To replace indicator rod and chain: Disconnect gears, replace part, and reconnect.

To replace trigger unit or cable: Detach cable at wheel end by loosening locknut and unscrewing adjusting sleeve. Then, push ferrule out of slot in (or unscrew from) trigger unit and pull it back. Put trigger on L or 3 and push cable in to detach it from trigger. Then, push trigger down even more and lift spring-held catch, and pull cable out. If you are replacing trigger unit, unscrew mounting bolts and it will come off. If you are replacing cable, loosen cable-housing clamp, and remove cable. Reverse procedure to reconnect. Adjust gears.

To adjust cable tension: Find the last clip on the frame holding cable housing at the point where wire becomes exposed. Loosen it and move it until the cable wire is snug, but not taut, when in H or 3.

Shimano

To adjust: Shift gears to N or 2. Then, loosen joint locknut and screw adjusting sleeve in or out until the N is centered in the window of bell-crank nut and thin line is in groove of nut. Retighten locknut and test gears.

To disconnect gears: Loosen joint locknut and detach cable by unscrewing adjusting sleeve. Then, unscrew bell-crank nut and pull push rod out of end of axle. Remove bell-crank locknut.

To reconnect gears: Screw bell-crank locknut well onto axle. Put push rod into end of axle. Then, screw bell-crank nut onto axle until there is a slight resistance. If bell-crank nut is not correctly positioned, unscrew it a partial turn until it is. Hold it in position and screw locknut tight against it. Put gear control unit on H or 3. Screw adjusting sleeve onto joint bolt a few turns. Shift to N or 2, and adjust.

To replace twist-grip or cable: Detach cable at wheel end by loosening joint locknut and unscrewing adjusting sleeve. Then, unscrew the two screws on twist grip being careful not to lose internal bearing and spring. Remove cable from twist grip. If you are replacing twist grip, you can pull it off. If you are replacing cable, loosen cable-housing clamp and remove cable. Reverse procedure to reassemble. Adjust gears.

To adjust cable tension: Find the last clip on the frame holding cable housing at the point where wire becomes exposed. Loosen it and move it until cable wire is snug, but not taut, when gears are in H or 3.

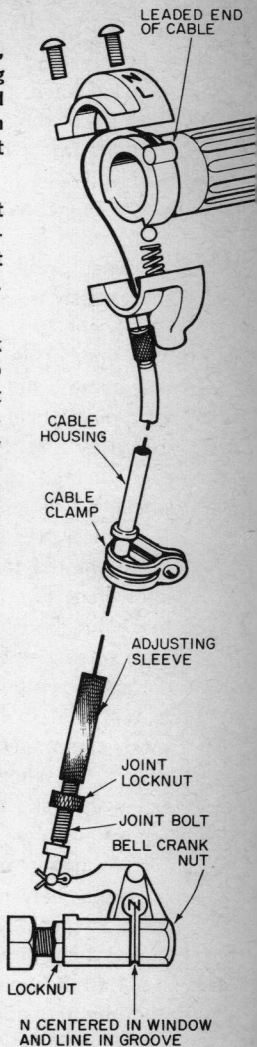

LEADED END OF CABLE

CABLE HOUSING

CABLE CLAMP

ADJUSTING SLEEVE

JOINT LOCKNUT

JOINT BOLT

BELL CRANK NUT

LOCKNUT

N CENTERED IN WINDOW AND LINE IN GROOVE

67

Gear Numbers and Speed

On early bikes, the pedals were mounted directly on the front wheel in the same way that they still are on a child's tricycle. Since the pedals and the wheel turned together, one turn of the pedals turned the wheel once. In order to go much faster than a person walking, bicycles had to be built with enormous front wheels—often measuring five feet (60 inches) in diameter. But the invention of the chain drive changed this. By putting the pedals on a gearwheel, which we call a sprocket, and connecting that sprocket by a closed chain to a smaller one on the back wheel, one turn of the pedals made the wheel turn more than once. This gave the cyclist a mechanical advantage that allowed him to go fast without the dangers of falling off a high wheel. A modern wheel, 27 inches in diameter, driven by a sprocket combination that turns it two times each pedal turn, covers the same distance that an old wheel, 60 inches in diameter, did in one turn.

Since a person considering a new chain-driven bike in 1890 wanted to know what size highwheeler it was the equivalent of, the custom developed of expressing this mechanical advantage in terms of the diameter of the old high wheel. And the modern bike which travels the same distance per pedal turn as an old 60-inch highwheeler is still said to have a 60-inch gear, although it is now more commonly expressed as a "gear of 60" or a "60 gear." You should note that this number is not the distance the bike travels but the diameter of an imaginary equivalent high wheel.

Although gear numbers can still be used to make comparisons between bikes, the development of variable gears, especially derailleur gears, makes an understanding of them important to the gear user. The gear ratio of most adult bikes can now be changed by pulling a lever, allowing the rider to handle differences in terrain, load, and other conditions.

The gear number of a bike—or for any combination of sprockets on a derailleur bike—can be calculated if you first count the number of teeth on each sprocket and find the diameter of your wheel (it's embossed on the tire). Then, use this formula (or table, next page):

$$\frac{\text{teeth in front sprocket}}{\text{teeth in rear sprocket}} \times \text{wheel diameter} = \text{gear number}$$

Example:

$$\frac{46 \text{ front teeth}}{18 \text{ rear teeth}} \times \quad 27 \text{ inches} = 69 \text{ gear}$$

This is a typical "normal" gear—a gear that will allow you to pedal easily on a flat paved surface without going too slowly. On most adult bikes, your back wheel will be turning two and a half times each pedal turn, and if you are pedaling at an average cadence of 60 pedal turns a minute, you will go 12 mph. The normal gear on most bikes is from 66 to 70. The middle gear of a 3-speed and the only gear of a single-speed is in this range.

A gear with a number lower than this is called a "low" gear. In a low gear, the back wheel on a full-size bike will turn from one and a quarter to two times each pedal turn —the equivalent of riding a relatively small 30- to 50-inch highwheeler. Since the bike becomes much easier to pedal, low gears are used to go up a hill without straining or to compensate for a heavy load or a head wind.

For speed, a "high" gear is needed. This is a gear which will turn the back wheel from three to four times each pedal turn—the equivalent of riding an impossibly large highwheeler, 80 to 100 inches in diameter. But the pedals are harder to turn, and most riders limit the use of high gears to going downhill when a bike has so much momentum that little effort is required to pedal.

Tables for finding gear numbers and speed follow.

Gear Number Chart

This chart gives gear numbers for most common sprocket sizes. If your sprockets aren't here, use the formula on p. 69. Once you have found your gear numbers, you can find speed and distance from the next chart.

	Number of teeth in front sprocket								
	27-inch diameter wheels							26-inch	
	39	40	45	46	49	50	52	46	52
14	75	77	87	89	94	96	100	85	97
15	70	72	81	83	88	90	94	80	90
16	66	67	76	77	83	84	88	75	84
17	62	63	71	73	78	79	83	70	79
18	58	60	67	69	73	75	78	66	75
19	55	57	64	65	70	71	74	63	71
20	53	54	61	62	66	67	70	60	68
21	50	51	58	59	63	64	67	57	64
22	48	49	55	56	60	61	64	54	61
23	46	47	53	54	57	59	61	52	59
24	44	45	51	52	55	56	58	50	56
25	42	43	49	50	53	54	56	48	54
26	40	41	47	48	51	52	54	46	52
28	38	39	43	44	47	48	50	43	48

Number of teeth in rear sprocket (row labels at left)

Example: A 10-speed bike with 27-inch wheels and 14-17-20-24-28-tooth rear sprockets and 39-52-tooth front sprockets has the gear combinations shown at the right. Arranged in sequence, they would be from low to high:

38-44-50-53-59-62-70-75-83-100

	Front	
Rear	39	52
14	75	100
17	62	83
20	53	70
24	44	59
28	38	50

On 3-speeds, you can only use this chart or the gear number formula to find normal gear. To get low gear, multiply normal gear by .75. To get high gear, multiply normal gear by 1.33. A table for a typical 3-speed is given on p. 64.

Speed and Distance

To figure speed, you have to know how fast you are pedaling. But once you have developed a natural pedaling rhythm, it's easy to count how often you turn the pedals a minute. Formulas for speed and distance are below.

Gear number	Distance each pedal turn	Number of pedal turns per minute			
		45 (slow)	60 (average)	75 (fast)	90 (very fast)
39	10¼ ft	5¼ mph	7 mph	8¾ mph	10½ mph
42	11	5¾	7½	9½	11½
45	11¾	6	8	10	12
48	12½	6½	8½	10¾	13
50	13	6¾	9	11	13½
53	14	7	9½	12	14
56	14½	7½	10	12½	15
59	15½	8	10½	13	16
61	16	8¼	11	13½	16½
65	17	8¾	11½	14½	17½
67	17½	9	12	15	18
70	18¼	9¼	12½	15¾	18½
73	19	9¾	13	16½	19½
75	19¾	10	13½	16¾	20
79	20½	10½	14	17¾	21
81	21	10¾	14½	18	21½
84	22	11¼	15	18¾	22½
87	22¾	11¾	15½	19½	23½
89	23½	12	16	20	24
93	24¼	12½	16½	20¾	25
95	24¾	12¾	17	21¼	25½
98	25½	13	17½	22	26
101	26½	13½	18	22½	27

Formulas: Inches traveled per pedal turn $= $ gear number $\times \dfrac{22}{7}$

To get feet divide by 12. Or, to get a figure in feet that is accurate within an inch or two, multiply gear number by .26.

$$\text{Speed(mph)} = \frac{\text{ft per pedal turn} \times \text{pedal turns per min.} \times 60}{5280}$$

Handlebars

Despite the plural name "handlebars," on most bikes there is only one piece of tubing. The shape of this tubing—more than anything else—determines the riding style. If the tubing is twisted up and back, the handlebars are "raised," and the rider holds the ends and assumes a more or less upright position. If the tubing is twisted forward, down, and back, the handlebars are "dropped," and the rider assumes any one of a number of forward-leaning positions, depending on where he grips the handlebars. These positions are discussed on p. 104.

Most handlebars and their stems—the post with a neck that holds the bars—are made of steel and chromed, but on many lightweights they are alloy.

The height and angle of handlebars should be adjusted to suit you. It is usually best to start by setting the height so the top of the stem is even with the top of the seat. Later, you may find it more comfortable to have them slightly higher or lower. But at least 2½ inches of the stem should be seated in the head tube. The angle is not very important on raised handlebars. But you may have to reset dropped handlebars a few times to find the most comfortable angle. It is usually recommended that the lower portion of the bars angle downward 10 degrees from horizontal, but the most important thing is that the position "feel right." Also, if your handlebars seem uncomfortably close or far away after you have had a chance to get used to them, you can replace the stem with one that has a longer or shorter extension. But check the horizontal position of the seat first (see p. 112). If you replace the stem or the handlebars, get the right size.

For safety, keep your handlebars tight and straight, keep the ends plugged or covered with grips, and replace loose grips. Taping dropped handlebars is optional, but it gives you a better grip and keeps your hands off metal on cold days.

Conventional

Raised handlebars are the most common on bikes with conventional features. They are also called "tourist" handlebars or "allrounders" because of their rider-surrounding shape.

Flat handlebars are similar to raised, but have less rise and little backturn. The rider has to lean more forward.

High-rise handlebars are used mostly on children's high-rise bikes. Their safety has been questioned because the child has less steering control with his hands so high. They are also used on some folding bikes and adult tricycles.

Dropped

The distance dropped handlebars bend forward is called the "throw." The distance they bend down is called the "drop." The forward projection of the stem is the "extension."

Maes handlebars are the most common of the square-shaped dropped handlebars. They are flat along the top and have a greater drop than throw.

Randonneur handlebars are similar to Maes, but they are slightly wider, have more throw, and bend up slightly along the top. They are popular for touring.

Narrow round-shaped dropped handlebars are used for track racing, but they are not comfortable for ordinary riding.

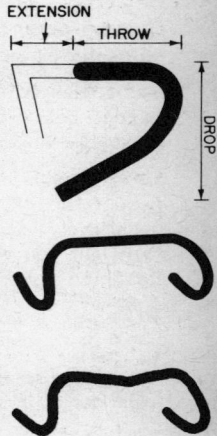

73

HANDLEBARS

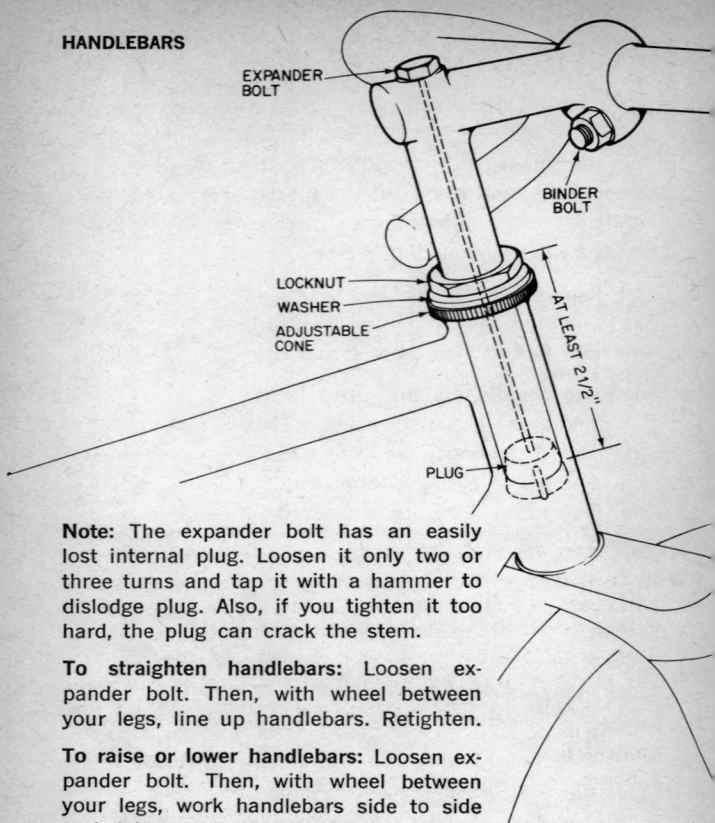

EXPANDER BOLT

BINDER BOLT

LOCKNUT
WASHER
ADJUSTABLE CONE

AT LEAST 2 1/2"

PLUG

Note: The expander bolt has an easily lost internal plug. Loosen it only two or three turns and tap it with a hammer to dislodge plug. Also, if you tighten it too hard, the plug can crack the stem.

To straighten handlebars: Loosen expander bolt. Then, with wheel between your legs, line up handlebars. Retighten.

To raise or lower handlebars: Loosen expander bolt. Then, with wheel between your legs, work handlebars side to side to height you want. Line up handlebars. Retighten bolt.

To adjust angle of handlebars: Loosen binderbolt,* reset angle, and retighten.

To tighten stem loose in frame: Tighten expander bolt. Check position first.

To remove handlebars from stem: Remove everything from handlebars. Loosen binderbolt.* Slide handlebars out.

* Stems with no extension have no binderbolt. On these, loosen the expander bolt.

74

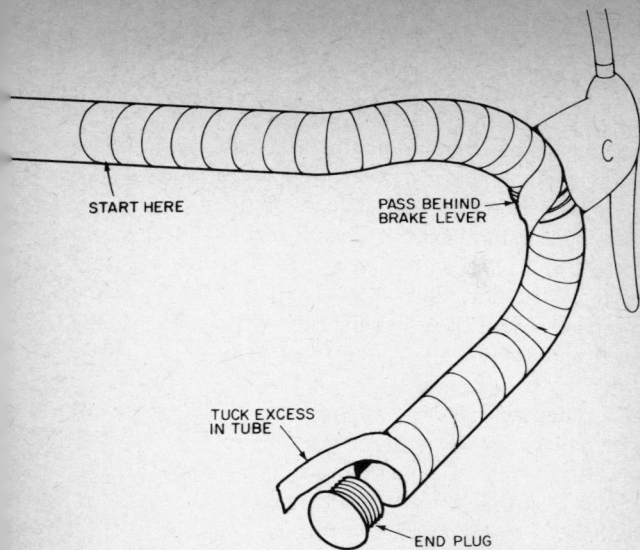

START HERE

PASS BEHIND BRAKE LEVER

C

TUCK EXCESS IN TUBE

END PLUG

To tape dropped handlebars: Before starting, remove end-plugs and old tapes and make sure brake levers are well positioned. You can use either adhesive or non-adhesive handlebar tape. Starting 1 to 3 inches from the stem, secure the end of the tape (with a bit of Scotch tape if necessary) and make two or three tight turns to keep the tape end in place. Then, spiral the tape out, overlapping about a ¼-inch. Tape behind brake lever and continue to the end. Cut off all but a couple of inches and shove the tape end into the handlebars and replace the plug. If you get a new endplug, be sure to get the right size. Most endplugs shove on and pry off, but some have a small screw which must be loosened first.

To replace grips: If old grips won't come off, cut them off. Filling the new grip with water and pouring it out will leave enough of a film of water so you can twist the new grip on.

If handlebars are hard to turn or if steering mechanism is loose in the frame, unscrew the locknut and adjust the cone. More details on pp. 95–98.

To remove handlebars and stem: Loosen expander bolt and work handlebars side to side until stem comes out. Now, if you want to replace the stem, take everything off one side of bars, loosen the binder bolt and slide the stem off.

Learning to Ride

If you don't know how, riding a bike may seem like an amazing feat of balance. And if you already know how and are trying to teach your child or a friend, it may seem so easy and natural that you can't understand why anyone can't just jump on a bike and go. Riding a bike is a balancing feat, but a simple one, and that is why nearly everyone can do it. It is less the rider who keeps the bike upright and balanced than the forward momentum. And in this, the bike is like a coin which will balance on its edge as long as it is kept rolling.

The major obstacle to getting a bike rolling for someone who has never ridden before is fear—fear of falling and fear of losing control and crashing into something. And the way to lessen these fears is not to try to convince yourself or someone else that they are unfounded, although that helps, but to actually reduce the chances of falling or crashing into something while learning.

The chances of falling, and the fear of it, can be almost eliminated by using a small bike. When seated on it, the beginner should have both feet—at least the balls of the feet—on the ground. For an adult, this means borrowing or renting a bike that is too small by ideal standards. It may be a child's bike with 24-inch wheels or an adult bike with 26-inch wheels and a small frame size (short seat tube) with the seat all the way down. A folding bike with the seat lowered can also be used. For a child, you can also borrow a smaller bike, but it's best for a child's first bike to be small. In addition, if the bike has an open (woman's) frame it's much easier to get on and off.

The chances of crashing into something can be reduced by simply choosing an open, empty paved area, such as a parking lot or school yard on a Sunday morning. An area with a very slight slope helps also, but is not necessary.

Whether you are teaching yourself or someone else, if you have a small bike and an open area, the procedure is simple. The first thing to be learned is to scoot the bike along by pushing with both feet at once. As the distances that can be scooted increase, a feel for balancing and steering a bike while it is in motion will develop. And after a few times, the feet will almost automatically come to rest on the pedals during long coasts. At this point, it's only a matter of starting to pedal. The first few rides will be wobbly, but as confidence grows, riding will become smoother.

Most adults can learn to ride this way the first day, and once an adult has gotten the feel of riding a bike, the transfer to the right size bike is easy, provided the seat is raised in stages as skill in riding increases. As it does, the chapter on riding techniques (p. 102) will be helpful, especially the part on getting on and off, which is something that may still cause trouble.

Children take longer, however, and it's best not to rush them. If you "want to get it over as quickly as possible," you'll find that ten-or fifteen-minute sessions every day will accomplish this faster and easier—for yourself and your child—than two-hour sessions on the weekends.

This method doesn't require anyone to hold up the bike or run along with it, and usually this kind of "help" only hinders learning. But a child may want this aid for reassurance. If you run along with him, grasp the rear of the seat so you can't be seen and so you can let go for short periods without it being noticed.

Training wheels are not recommended. With them, a child doesn't learn to balance; instead, he learns to throw his weight onto an outside wheel. Parents who want their child to learn to ride should remove them before he becomes dependent on them.

Lights and Night Riding

Riding at night can be very pleasant. There is less traffic, and during the heat of summer it is often the only time when it is cool enough to ride. But riding at night requires extra care. Here are some suggestions:

Make sure you can be seen. A rear reflector that can be seen for 300 feet and a headlight that can be seen for 500 feet is required by law on bikes ridden at night in nearly all areas. But this is a bare minimum. If you ride much at night, you should install a rear light and put bands or spirals of reflective tape on your bike so it can be seen from the rear and the sides. And if you wear clothing that is light and bright in color you will increase your visibility. A bright yellow windbreaker or a reflective safety vest or belt is a good investment.

Although the primary function of a headlight is to warn cars and pedestrians, on dark country roads and poorly lit streets it will help you see the road surface. Focus it far enough ahead so that you will have time to stop for or veer around obstacles.

Choose your route carefully. If you stick to streets and roads that you know, you can anticipate intersections, driveways, and rough spots. If you know that a street is poorly lit or filled with potholes, gravel, or glass, try to avoid it. And in urban areas, avoid deserted side streets and parks at night. Although you should always try to avoid heavy or fast traffic, at night you can safely use many well-lit main thoroughfares.

Ride more slowly than you do during the day. Give yourself time to stop if the unexpected happens.

Dusk is dangerous for cyclists because of the generally poor visibility—especially in late fall and early spring when dusk and rush hour coincide. If you use your bike for commuting, put your light on for extra safety.

Lights are available in a variety of styles, but the perfect light for bikes hasn't been invented yet. There are two types: battery lights and generator lights.

Battery lights are variants of the ordinary flashlight and most are not of good enough quality to withstand hard bike use. Contacts and switches jar loose and rust shut, the cases pop open, and the batteries corrode if not replaced frequently. All of these give you no light when you need it. But if you get a battery light that clips on so that it can be removed for daytime riding, and if you don't use heavy rechargeable batteries (which tend to flatten contacts), you can avoid many of these problems.

Generator lights are run by a small generator, or dynamo, on the wheel. They have none of the problems of battery lights—and give you the satisfaction of generating your own electricity. But the light becomes dimmer when you slow down and goes out when you stop; and the generator puts a slight drag on the wheel, which can be tiring on a long night ride. Both a front and a rear light can be run off a generator.

A small strap-on flashlight with a white front light and red rear light makes a good auxilliary light. It is lightweight and is strapped to the arm or the calf. On the calf, it is particularly noticeable because it will move up and down as you pedal.

Reflectors should be large and marked "approved"—which means they can be seen from 300 feet. On bikes without fenders, they can be mounted on the carrier, between the seat stays, or hung from the seat.

Reflective tape is cheap and easy to apply. Use red on the rear and sides and yellow or white on the front. It can be seen best if it is put on in stripes, bands, or spirals that form an alternating pattern.

Locking your Bike

Whenever you park your bike—even if it is only for a few minutes—you should lock it. How securely you lock it will depend on what kind of bike you have. If you have a beat-up old middleweight, it's not likely to be stolen, and you can probably get away with a light cable lock that provides only symbolic protection. But on most bikes you need real protection in the form of a strong chain and lock. If you have an expensive lightweight, it's best never to leave it unattended. Even if the bike is locked well, you can lose some very expensive parts. If you have a lightweight that just looks expensive, you need to lock it very well, too, since you can't expect every thief to be a connoisseur.

When you lock your bike, you should put the chain around a strong stationary object and pass it through the frame and the back wheel, since they are the two most expensive parts of your bike. If you have a front wheel with a quick-release front hub or with butterfly wing axle nuts, you can do one of three things to keep it from being taken: lock the wheel with a small auxilliary lock or cable, which is good; take the wheel off and chain it up with the back wheel and the frame, which is better; or take it with you, which is best. If you have a folding bike, the only secure way to chain it to something is to fold it and put the chain through both wheels and around the seat tube.

The best place to lock your bike is where you can see it. If you can't, the next best place is a public area where anyone tampering with it would be conspicuous. Most bike racks are in public places, with other cyclists coming and going. And if you have an inexpensive bike, the odds are very low that your bike will be stolen with more expensive bikes around. The only way to lock your bike securely to a bike rack is to put the rear wheel in the rack and pass the chain through the wheel, the rear stays, and the rack. To do this, you need a long chain, which will be heavy. With a shorter chain you can securely lock your bike to a parking sign, a tree, a fence post, or a metal railing. Avoid anything as short as a parking meter where someone only has to lift your bike up to detach it.

The best protection is a case-hardened chain with links at least ⅜-inch thick. These chains are expensive and heavy but almost impossible to cut. Since these chains vary in quality, test one with a hack saw or a file; it should barely scratch the finish. To cut down on weight, get one that's only 24 inches long—just long enough to go through the frame and back wheel and around a narrow post or pipe. Be sure to cover it so it won't scratch up your bike. An old inner tube is recommended.

The next best protection is an ordinary strong link chain of similar size from your local hardware store. These chains can be cut, but only a pro with a giant pair of cutters or an amateur with a hack saw and a lot of time can do it. Again, you should cover the chain, but since it is lighter, you can have a longer chain. A 36-inch piece will go around larger posts.

Whichever kind of chain you get, the weak link will be the lock, unless you get a lock of comparable quality. The best are large, solid, and have case-hardened hasps. Combination locks, in general, are not recommended. With most, it is not too difficult to figure out the combination, and on cold days, they have a tendency to jam. On the other hand, no key-lock is totally pick-proof.

The lighter plastic-covered chains and "airplane" cables that are sold for bikes can be cut with a bolt cutter. Traditional bike locks with long hasps and other locks that attach only to the bike are not recommended. It's easy to lift up the locked wheel and roll the bike off. But any of these is good as an extra lock for the front wheel.

Maintenance and Repair

Routine Maintenance

Routine maintenance consists of little more than tightening any loose nuts or bolts on your bike, cleaning it, and adjusting and oiling its moving parts. Occasionally, you may want to wax it or you may have to make a simple repair or replace a worn or damaged part. Even if you are not mechanically adept, you needn't shy away from this because your bike is a simple machine. In return for little effort, you will get many miles of safer, smoother, trouble-free riding.

The amount of routine maintenance will vary with the kind of bike you have. In general, the fancier your bike is, the more exposed—and vulnerable—parts it will have and the more maintenance it will need. A complete maintenance chart is given on the following pages and the procedure outlined in it shouldn't take more than a half-hour on most bikes—an hour at most on derailleur lightweights. This chart gives a thorough list for going over your bike, but you don't need to be that thorough every time you check your bike. Usually, it takes only 10 to 15 minutes to tighten any loose bolts, to wipe your bike off, to check your brakes and gears, and to oil them and the hubs and chain.

If you ride frequently, it is recommended that you do this once a month. The only thing that needs more frequent attention is the air pressure in your tires, which should be checked every few days. Then, use the maintenance chart to give your bike a thorough checkout every few months. In addition, it is recommended that you give your bike a complete going over when you first get it, at the beginning of the riding season, and before you go on a long tour. If you ride a lot in the rain or on bumpy, dusty roads, you will need to check your bike more frequently and also to wipe off moisture and dirt after each use.

Of course, every time you ride you should be on the alert for any sign that something is wrong—especially a strange noise. If you hear a clattering, klacking, rattling, whizzing, or cracking noise, find the cause and fix it. Any trouble your bike develops should not be put off; it will only get worse.

Since most bikes are very durable, most riders don't think about maintenance until something goes wrong. Bikes that have been neglected develop problems that can make the first maintenance job a major undertaking. Even if nothing is broken, parts may be rusted or frozen on and the end threads of bolts may be damaged, making it hard to get a nut on or off. By then the bike usually needs a complete overhaul, not just a routine checking. The procedure for overhauling bearing parts is given on p. 95 and for cleaning derailleur parts on p. 53. But if you are new to mechanical undertakings and your bike needs more than routine work, you'll probably prefer to have your bike overhauled by a good bike shop the first time. Of course, if you have a new bike, you can save yourself a lot of trouble if you keep it up from the start.

Except for an occasional flat tire, your bike should very rarely need a major repair if you keep it up and ride with reasonable care.

Storing your bike properly is good preventive maintenance. The most important thing is to keep it dry. When you are not using your bike, it should be inside. If it is impossible to keep it inside, you can get a bike cover or a tarp to put over it, but it's a poor substitute. If you put your bike away for the winter, give it a thorough cleaning and oiling first. If you hang it upside down from hooks, it will extend the life of the tires. And if you wrap it in plastic, it will keep out both moisture and dirt.

Mechanical Tips

1 **Clockwise tightens** and **counterclockwise loosens** all parts of your bike except for the left pedal and the left crank housing, which are the reverse.

2 Don't tighten any part on a bike too hard. You can shear off the threads or bend a part and, in some cases, getting a replacement is difficult or expensive. Be especially careful if you are working on lightweight alloy parts or if you are using a tool with a lot of leverage. Also, remember that some parts, such as the pivotal bolts on brake rim units and the cones in bearing parts should be tightened and then backed off.

3 Metric nuts and bolts are used on all imported bikes and on imported parts of American-made bikes, which includes all gears and hand brakes. Any nonadjustable wrench you use on these bikes or parts should be metric. And, if you lose a metric nut, you can't replace it with an inch-threaded one. It won't fit on the metric bolt. But you can usually replace both the nut and bolt. Of course, if you lose a metric part that screws onto the bike, such as an axle nut, you have to get an exact replacement. Bike shops carry metric parts and tools.

4 If you replace a bolt with a new longer one, cut it after it is installed. It's often impossible to get a nut on over damaged threads at the end of a bolt.

5 Don't force any part on if it won't go on easily. Stop and try to figure out why it won't.

6 If a part is "frozen" or rusted on, put a little penetrating oil (such as Liquid Wrench) on it, tap it a few times to work the oil in, and then let it set for a few minutes before you try to move it again. If this doesn't work after a couple of tries, go to a bike shop.

Notes on Cleaning and Oiling

Solvent is sometimes needed to remove the old oil and grit from moving parts before you reoil them. You can use kerosine, diesel fuel, or gasoline. All of them are highly inflammable, and when you use them, have good ventilation and don't smoke. Gasoline is especially dangerous; avoid using it if you can. Don't get solvent on the tires. It corrodes rubber.

Oils vary in viscosity—in how thick they are. For most parts of your bike, a very light oil is all that is needed, and a household oil like Three-in-One is fine, although special bicycle oils are sold in bike shops. For hubs with oil fittings, a slightly thicker motor oil (SAE no. 20 or 30, but nothing thicker) is recommended, but the lighter oil can also be used. A spray oil is useful for the hard-to-get-at parts of a derailleur. Always wipe off all excess oil. It picks up dirt.

Grease is needed if you overhaul a bearing part (see p. 95). A light white grease such as Lubriplate, Gold Medal, or Schwinn's Cycle Lube is recommended.

Cleaning of the frame, fenders, wheels, handlebars, and seat should be done only with a damp cloth. Never use soap, detergent, or large amounts of water on your bike. The chain drive should be cleaned only with a solvent.

Wax your bike with a bicycle wax. Avoid polishes that contain abrasives—such as car polish. Regular use of an abrasive polish will ruin the finish of your bike, but if you have a bike in bad shape, a polish can be used once to clean it up.

Saddle soap is needed for leather seats.

On bikes with rim brakes, don't wax the rims and don't get oil on them or on the brake shoes because it will make your brakes slip.

Tools

Having the right tools can save you a lot of time and frustration and save your bike a lot of unnecessary damage. But if you rush out and buy every tool you think you might need or every tool that strikes your fancy in a bike shop, you can spend a lot of money. Most of the routine work on a bike can be done with a screwdriver and a wrench (or a set of them) and some tire tools. Since other tools are specialized, are only needed occasionally, and are not needed on all bikes, buy these tools only as you need them. If you have an expensive bike, however, you are more likely to need specialized tools.

Get the right tools. Make sure that any tool you are using fits snugly on the part you are fixing. If a screwdriver is too small for a slot, it will distort the slot. If a wrench is slightly too large for a nut, it will round the edges of the nut. And in both cases, it will make future adjustments impossible.

Here are some recommendations on tools:

Screwdrivers: One with a blade about 5 inches long and with a ¼-inch tip will take care of most needs and is easy to carry. At home, it may be useful to have a larger or a smaller one, depending on your bike.

Crescent wrench: This adjustable wrench can be used on any bike. But if the jaws are not always adjusted to fit a nut snugly, you can round the edges. A 6-inch one is best.

Bike spanner wrench: A variety of these easy-to-carry flat wrenches are made. The most common type (shown below) has openings that fit most common metric nuts and hub cones. The large curve fits the bottom-bracket lockring.

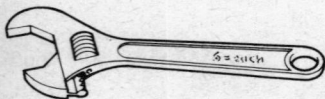

CRESCENT WRENCH   BIKE SPANNER

Ordinary wrenches: Open or box wrenches that you may already have in inch sizes can be used on American-made bikes.

Cable cutters: Strong ones with V-shaped jaws are better than cutting pliers. But you can use pliers if you are careful to install the cable before cutting.

Hammer: Needed mostly for adjusting handlebars. Always put a piece of wood between the hammer and the bike and just tap.

File: Needed occasionally; e.g., for filing off spoke heads.

For Tires

Bike tire irons: Two or three of these small irons are useful for removing high-pressure conventional tires (see p. 118).

Pump: The larger foot-held manual pump is better than the small tubular pump. But the small pump is needed for touring.

Air-pressure gauge: An extra, but it will pay for itself if it saves you one blowout from overinflating an inner tube.

For Wheels

Spoke wrench: For adjusting spokes (see p. 136).

Cone wrenches: Flat thin wrenches that fit the cones on the hub if bike spanner doesn't. Get the right size.

For Derailleurs

Set of metric bike wrenches: These light stamped-out wrenches are essential for adjusting gears and brakes on derailleurs.

Chain rivet tool: Needed to remove and repair chain (p. 59).

Freewheel tool: Needed to remove freewheel (see p. 58).

Cotterless crank tool: Needed only on better bikes (p. 99).

Other: On some derailleurs, a Phillips screwdriver to fit X-slotted screws or Allen wrenches to fit set screws are needed.

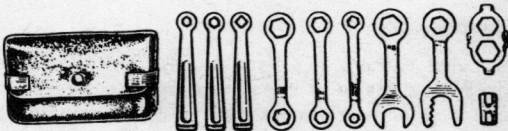

METRIC WRENCH SET

Maintenance Guide

A suggested procedure for going over your bike is given on these pages. The left pages cover tightening and adjusting, and there are page references to the sections on the parts if you find anything wrong. The right pages give the details on cleaning and oiling for the corresponding parts. If you are checking your bike for the first time, read the first part of this chapter.

With your bike upright:

Tightening and adjusting

Frame and fenders pages 42 and 134

Shake the bike. If a fender or chainguard (or anything else) rattles, tighten it.

Look for any obvious damage and also for not-so-obvious bent tubes or fork.

Handlebars page 72

Both stem and handlebars should be attached tightly. Worn or loose grips or handlebar tape should be replaced.

With front hand brake on, rock bike back and forth to see if there is play in the steering head. Also, make sure that the handlebars turn smoothly.

Seat page 110

Should be tight and straight. Replace a worn seat. Reassess whether height is correct for you.

Accessories page 16

Check that carriers, kickstands, bells, and other extras are tight. With lights, also check that batteries are strong and uncorroded or that generator is well attached. Check for loose or broken reflectors or mirrors.

You will probably find it easier to clean and oil a part while you are working on it and then at the end to wipe over the entire bike to remove any smudges or oil. If you wax, it should be done when you are completely through. Notes on cleaning and oiling are given on p. 87. Be very careful not to get solvent or oil on the tires.

Cleaning and oiling

Wipe entire bike, except chain drive, with a damp cloth.

Scratches on the frame or fenders can be covered with auto or bike touch-up paint.

The frame and fenders can be waxed to preserve finish.

Waxing exposed parts will help prevent rusty handlebars. If they are in bad shape, you can use a chrome polish.

If steering is stiff, headset may need to be overhauled and regreased (see p. 95).

Saddle soap leather seats; wipe others off with a damp cloth.

Spray chromed accessories, such as lights and bells, with a clear spray enamel when you first get them. Then, just wipe them off along with the rest of the bike. Woven wood baskets can also be sprayed to preserve them.

If your bike has gears or hand brakes, also check:

(If your bike doesn't have them, go on to the next page.)

Tightening and adjusting

Cables

Cables are often the source of gear and brake trouble. New cables, especially, tend to stretch and need to be taken up at the wheel end. Check old cable wires and housings for wear, and replace cables with more than one broken strand.

Hand brakes   page 22

Levers should be tightly attached. When you squeeze them, they should move about 2 inches and not touch handlebars. Their position should be comfortable and easily reached.

Rim brake units should grab the rims evenly and smoothly and spring back. They should be centered.

Brake shoes should be ⅛- to ³⁄₁₆-inch from rim and lined up with it. They should be tight and not worn.

Hub (3-speed) gears   page 62

Selector should click easily into all gears.

Check position of the indicator in the window of the long tubular nut on the right rear axle. Adjust if needed.

Derailleur gears   page 46

With your bike upside down or on a rack, test the entire range of gears while turning pedals. It should work smoothly on every sprocket. Pay special attention to the highest and lowest gears. Also, check that:

Changers are well attached, work smoothly, and aren't bent.

Freewheel has no worn or bent teeth.

Selector lever(s) move easily, but aren't loose.

Cleaning and oiling

Put a few drops of light oil on cables at the points where they enter the cable housing. When you replace a cable wire, put a light coat of grease on part that will be inside the housing.

Put a drop of light oil on the pivotal points of the brake levers.

Put a couple of drops of light oil on pivotal bolts of rim units and at the point where the spring rubs the arms.

Remove embedded grit in shoes. If rubber has burned onto rims, it can be cleaned off with a little solvent.

Put a drop of light oil on pivotal part of selector unit.

Lightly oil indicator chain (or moving parts of Shimano gears). Put a tablespoon of motor oil in nipple on rear hub, or three or four good squirts of a light oil.

Wipe off grit and dirt on all parts of the system. Clean and oil chain as described on next page. Use solvent to clean part if very dirty. Then, using a light oil or a spray lubricant (which is good for hard-to-get-at parts):

Lightly oil all moving parts of both changers.

Lightly oil the freewheel. (Every six months, remove freewheel, flush with solvent and reoil.)

Don't put oil on levers; they work on friction.

With your bike upside down or on a rack:
(Don't let the bike rest on brake or gear levers. If necessary, you can put it on its left (non-chain) side on cardboard.)

Tightening and adjusting

Wheels page 132

Both wheels should spin freely with little or no side play.

Axle nuts (or quick-releases) should be tight.

Check for broken or loose spokes. Make sure wheel isn't warped.

Tires page 114

Check inflation. Valve stem should be straight.

Check for wear, cuts, cracks, and embedded particles.

Pedals page 100

Both should be tightly screwed into crank. Both should spin freely but not have any side play. On rubber pedals, treads should not be worn; tread rods may need tightening.

Crank page 95

Should turn easily without any side play. On three-piece cranks, make sure that crank arms are not loose.

Chain page 30

Chain should have only about ½-inch play up or down.

To check if old chain is worn, grab top and bottom of chain and pull it tight around the front sprocket. If you can lift more than ½ inch off the sprocket, replace it.

Coaster brakes page 29

Check that brake arm is tightly secured to the clip on stay.

Turn pedals rapidly forward, then reverse. Wheel should stop instantly.

Cleaning and oiling

Put a half teaspoon of motor oil, or two or three squirts of light oil in the oil fitting of the front hub, if there is one. If wheel doesn't spin freely, hub may need overhaul (p. 95).

Wax unchromed spokes to prevent rust. Don't wax the rims if you have rim brakes.

Keep solvent and oil off the tires. They corrode the rubber.

Remove dust cap and squirt a little light oil into the pedals. If pedals don't spin freely, they may need overhauling (p. 95) or replacement.

If the crank doesn't turn easily, it may need overhauling (p. 95).

Clean chain by running it through a rag soaked in solvent a few times. Then after it dries, put a drop of light oil on each roller as you turn the pedals. Wipe off excess oil. If chain is grimy, remove it, soak in solvent, and reoil.

Put a tablespoon of motor oil, or three or four squirts of light oil in the oil fitting on the rear hub. New hubs are packed with grease and don't need oil for first year or so.

Complex Repairs

The next few pages cover the overhauling and fixing of the internal bearing parts of your bike. Most people can handle these repairs. Other complex repairs, however, should be undertaken with caution. If you are an average rider, you will find it easier and probably cheaper in the long run to take any repair not covered in this book to a bike mechanic who has the tools and experience to handle it. But if you are mechanically inclined and you are fairly certain, for example, that it is a prong in your freewheel that is jammed or a brake arm that needs to be filed a bit to work smoothly, you can dismantle the part and try to fix it. Here are some hints:

1 Before you take anything apart, try cleaning, oiling, and adjusting it. With most parts the best way to clean them is to flush them out with a solvent.

2 Price any part you plan to take apart. If it's cheap to replace it, the part is not worth fixing.

3 If only a small part of a mechanism is broken, it is often impossible to get a replacement part separately.

4 Before you take something apart, be sure you understand how it works. Logic is often your best tool in getting a part to work.

5 Remember the exact sequence in which you dismantle a part so you can put it back together the same way. If you do have trouble remembering, take a look at the same part on another bike like yours.

6 Don't dismantle any part more than you have to.

7 If a metal part is bent and you straighten it, it will never be as strong as it was.

8 Don't under any circumstances take apart the rear hub of a bike with a coaster brake or hubchanger gears. These hubs are the only really complex parts used on bikes.

Overhauling and Fixing Bearing Parts

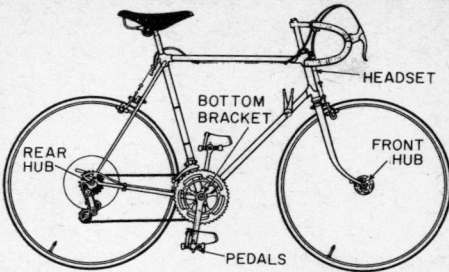

At the center of every major moving part of your bike—inside the hubs of the wheels, inside the pedals, and inside the frame at the points where the bike is pedaled and steered—small hard-steel balls (ball bearings) are used to reduce friction and to give you a smoother ride.

For your bike to work most efficiently, these parts periodically need to be overhauled—taken apart, cleaned with solvent, and packed with grease. How often depends on how much you ride, but for hubs and pedals once a year is recommended and for the headset and bottom bracket, every two years.

Also, occasionally something goes wrong with one of these parts. It may simply be that the part binds and won't spin freely or that it wiggles and has too much play. Both of these problems often can be corrected by adjustment. But sometimes adjustment doesn't work or something more serious may be wrong; a cracking sound, for example, is the surest sign of a broken bearing. And in these cases, the part has to be overhauled.

Most riders will recoil at the idea of even touching these greasy, dirty, and seemingly complex parts of their bikes. And many will prefer to have their bike serviced. But if you have been taking care of your bike regularly you should be able to handle these enclosed parts.

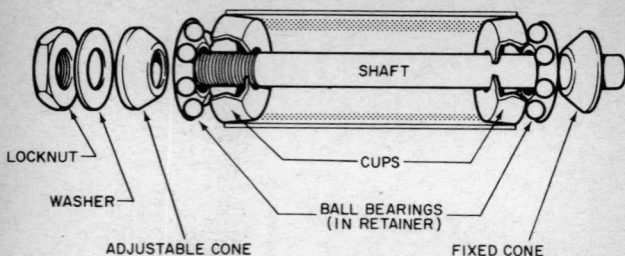

All bearing fittings are similar. They are used only where there is a revolving shaft or parts revolving about a shaft. At either end of the shaft, there is a set of ball bearings. And each set of bearings is squeezed between a cone on the shaft and a cup on the housing. Usually, both of the cups and one of the cones are fixed and are not easily moved. But the other cone can be screwed in or out along the shaft to adjust the pressure on both sets of bearings. Once this adjustable cone is set, a locknut is tightened against it to keep it from moving. There is usually a washer between the cone and the locknut.

The setup will vary slightly from bike to bike and from fitting to fitting. You may find that the cups are not just hard to remove but a permanent part of the housing and the fixed cone a permanent part of the shaft. On American-made bikes, the ball bearings will be set in a ring called a retainer or a cage, but on imported bikes or parts, they are usually loose and set in dustcaps to keep dirt out. The bottom bracket on imported bikes has other differences which are explained on p. 99.

The general procedures for adjusting and overhauling all parts with bearings are the same and are given here. Notes on the individual parts are given on the following pages. If you decide to do your own overhauls, it's best to learn with a pedal. If you give up or mess it up, it's easy to replace.

To adjust cone: All you have to do is screw the adjustable cone in or out. But to get to it, the locknut has to be loosened and backed off (or removed) first. In adjusting, the idea is to have the cone tight enough so that there is no play but not so tight that the part doesn't rotate freely. If there is too much play in the part, tighten the cone snugly —but not too hard—against the bearings. Then, back it off a quarter-turn at a time until the part rotates freely. If the part binds, you only need to back the cone off. It usually takes a few tries before you get it right. Once it is, hold the adjustable cone in place to keep it from moving and tighten the locknut against it. On most bikes, you will have to accept a bit of side play to get the part rotating freely, but on precision-made lightweights, you shouldn't have any.

To overhaul: So that you can get the parts back in right, you have to observe closely and remember the sequence in which you remove them. Start by removing the locknut, washer, and adjustable cone. Then, remove the first set of bearings. If they are in a retainer, they will come right out. But if they are in a dust cap, or just loose, be ready to catch all of them. Count them and note the number. You can tell you've lost one if both sets in the fitting don't have the same number or if there is a lot of space between the balls when you replace them. At this point, the shaft can be pulled out from the other side along with the fixed cone and the other set of bearings (but remember to catch loose bearings).

Soak all of the parts in a solvent, such as kerosine, to clean them, and flush out the housing with the same solvent. After they are cleaned and wiped off, inspect the bearings and the parts in direct contact with them. Any bearing or other part that is damaged, worn, or pitted should be replaced with an exact replacement.

If the bearings are in a retainer, fill the retainer with a light, white bicycle grease such as Lubriplate, Gold Medal, or Schwinn's Cycle Lube. If the bearings are loose, set them in a heavy coat of this grease in the dust cap. But don't overdo the grease. It picks up dirt.

Everything should be replaced exactly as it came out. The flat side of the retainer goes against the cone. At the end, the adjustable cone should be set as described above.

Pedals: The locknut and the adjustable cone are on the outside. You have to pry off or unscrew a dust cap to get to them (see p. 101). Remove pedal before overhauling.

Front hub: The adjustable cone is usually on the left (non-chain) side, but sometimes both cones are adjustable or the wheel has been reversed. The adjustable cone has two flattened edges which a thin flat wrench or bike spanner will fit on. If both cones are adjustable, work only on one. On some bikes, the axle nut serves as the locknut. (See p. 134.) The cups are usually a permanent part of the hub. When the bearings are properly adjusted, a wheel should rotate from just the weight of the valve stem. The cone should be adjusted with the wheel on the bike, but to overhaul, the wheel has to be removed.

Rear hub: Hubs that contain internal gears or coaster brakes are too complex to be adjusted or overhauled by anyone other than a mechanic. Even adjusting them affects the function of the gears and brakes. Derailleur hubs can be overhauled the same as front hubs once the freewheel has been removed (see p. 56). But since the hub is not centered on the axle, leave right cone on to find hub position.

Headset (steering head): The upper tube of the fork is the rotating shaft in this case. The locknut and the adjustable cone are located at the point where the handlebar stem enters the fork tube (see p. 74). The adjustable cone usually has a finely ridged edge like a coin and can be turned by hand. To overhaul, remove everything from the fork: the handlebars, the wheel, the fender, and the rim brake. The cups are hard to remove and usually there is no need to.

Bottom bracket on one-piece (American) crank: The locknut and adjustable cone are on the left (non-chain) side and are reverse threaded (loosen clockwise). The adjustable cone has a slotted head and can be loosened with a screwdriver. To overhaul, first remove the chain and chainguard on the right side (p. 31 or 57) and the pedal on the left side (p. 101). The locknut, adjustable cone, and left bearings can be slid off the left crank. Then, the crank can be worked out through the right side. The other bearings and the sprocket will come off with it. The cups are hard to remove and should be left alone. The bearings have retainers.

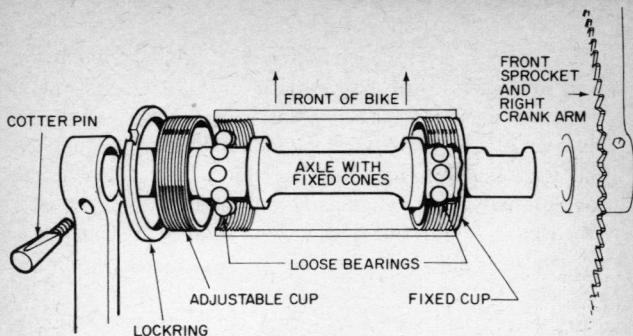

Bottom bracket of three-piece (imported) crank: The setup is the reverse of other fittings. The cones are inside, fixed on the axle. The cups are outside, screwed into the frame, and the one on the left (non-chain) side is adjustable. Instead of a locknut, it has a lockring. The lockring and adjustable cup loosen clockwise (the reverse of other parts).

Before overhauling, remove the crank arms (see below). The chain will come off when you remove the right crank arm and the attached front sprocket. The bearings are loose; don't work on the bike upside down or you may lose a bearing in the frame tubes. In overhauling, first remove lockring, adjustable cup, and left bearings. Then pull the axle out, and put your finger in to get the right bearings out. The right cup should be left alone. When you replace the right bearings, set them in a coat of grease on the axle. The left bearings should be set in the cup.

To remove cottered crank arms: Each crank arm is held onto the axle by a cotter pin, a tapered bolt. First, screw the nut to the end of the cotter pin to protect threads. Then, supporting the crank with a piece of hardwood, tap the pin loose with a hammer. Remove nut and pin. Always support crank and never hit hard or else you may damage bearings or cups. When you replace the pin, the flat side goes toward the axle. Tap the pin in with the same caution, and then replace the nut. Don't tighten nut to pull the pin in.

To remove cotterless crank arms: Each crank arm is held on by a bolt into the end of the axle and is usually covered by a dust cap. A special tool is needed to remove the bolt.

Pedals

There are two types of pedals: rubber pedals, which are used on bikes with conventional features, and metal "rattrap" pedals, used on bikes with racing features. A wide variety of both types is made. Rubber pedals are fine for casual riding, but they don't hold your feet in position very well, especially on hills, and eventually, they will wear out and have to be replaced. If you ride a lot, live in a hilly area, or tour, metal rattrap pedals are better. They are designed to save weight and energy, to grip better, and to last longer. Unlike rubber pedals, which usually have a platform that can be disassembled and sometimes needs to be tightened, the rattrap pedals have a one-piece platform, often made of an alloy to save weight. The teeth along the edges of the platform vary from very sharp to blunt. The sharp ones grip your shoe better, but can dig into the soles and catch on your clothing. Many rattraps come with toe clips and straps to hold the ball of your foot on the pedal—or you can add them. But only experienced riders should use them. Getting out of them in an emergency is an art.

All pedals should spin freely without any side play. If the platform is too tight or too loose, not only is a lot of energy lost in the pedal, but the bearings inside the pedal will be quickly damaged. If your pedal makes a gracking noise, the bearings may already be damaged. If oiling and readjusting don't help, it is better to replace rubber pedals, but if you have good rattrap pedals, you may want to overhaul them (see p. 96). When you replace the pedals, take your bike with you to be sure the new pedals have threads that fit the crank. Remember that the left (non-chain side) pedal is one of the few parts on your bike that has reverse threading. It screws off clockwise and screws on counterclockwise. Look for an L or R on the spindle. Be careful not to damage the threads of the crank by forcing on the wrong pedal.

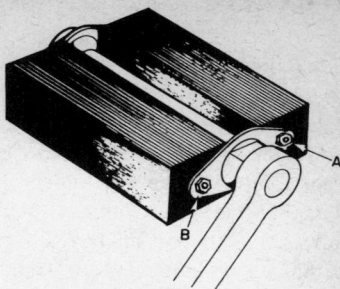

To remove, replace, or tighten pedal: Use a thin, flat wrench (or bike spanner) that will fit on the spindle between the pedals and the crank. The left pedal removes clockwise and is replaced or tightened counterclockwise. The right pedal loosens counterclockwise and tightens clockwise. Be careful not to damage the threads.

To tighten rubber pads: Tighten nuts A and B.

To adjust pedal with side play or one that is hard to turn: Remove dust cap, which will either screw or pry off.* Loosen the locknut and spin it back and pull back washers, if any. If pedal has side play, tighten the cone and back it off a quarter turn. If pedal is hard to turn, loosen the cone a quarter turn. Put a few drops of light oil in the bearing and spin pedal. Repeat until the pedal spins freely. Tighten locknut and replace dust cap. (For more, see pp. 95–98).

* If your rubber pedal doesn't have a dust cap, remove nuts A and B and pull off the platform to get to the locknut.

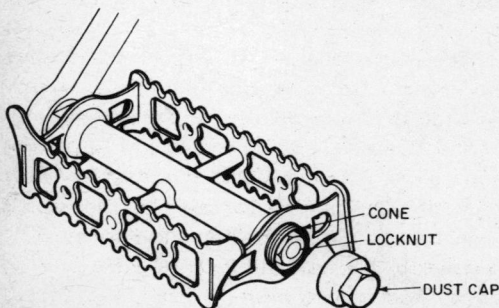

101

Riding Technique

Since the "engine" running your bike is your body, riding technique is much more than simply steering. It also involves how you hold yourself on the bike, how you pedal, how often you pedal, and how you use your brakes and gears. All of these will affect the efficient translation of your muscle power into a mechanical momentum that can be maintained for hours.

An inexperienced rider tends to sit upright, grip the handlebars tightly, tense up, put his insteps on the pedals, and pump them up and down slowly. This will get the bike going, but the rider will be exhausted if he goes for any distance. By contrast, look at the effortless, graceful way a good cyclist uses his bike. You may be tempted to dismiss it as a smooth "style," but the inexperienced rider would do well to try to emulate this style. Tests have shown that the experienced rider is using only half as much energy as the inexperienced rider.

Specific suggestions for developing a good riding style are given on the following pages, but just relaxing and trying to imitate the grace of a good cyclist will do wonders for your riding efficiency and greatly improve your control, balance, and comfort. And it will help you to develop a feel for riding as one smooth, coordinated activity—which is what the sum of the separate techniques should be.

Adjusting your bike to fit you is a prerequisite to riding well. The height of the seat and the handlebars are particularly important, and it may also be necessary to adjust the tilt of both and to move the seat back or forth. Adjustments for seats are given on p. 112 and for handlebars on p. 72. The most efficient position for the seat is quite high. You may want a slightly lower height if you ride in traffic or only ride for short trips, since it is much easier to get on and off quickly. If you have just learned or relearned to ride, keep it low.

Braking

For safety, learning to brake properly is more important than any other riding technique. Except for emergencies, you should always avoid stopping suddenly. If you look ahead and anticipate intersections, rough spots in the road, or cars pulling out or stopping, you will usually have plenty of time to bring your bike to a slow and safe stop. The faster you are going the more important it is to have time to slow the bike by gently applying the brakes before you have to stop.

On most adult bikes, there are brakes on both wheels and you should use both, applying them evenly. Using the front brake alone can throw you onto or over the handlebars, and using the rear brake alone can cause you to skid and lose control.

When you use your brakes to slow your bike, as on a long downhill coast, do not apply them continuously unless you are going so fast that you must to maintain control. On any brakes, continuous friction wears out the brake shoes. With hand brakes, it can burn rubber onto the rims, which will make the brakes grab too quickly, and it may heat up the inner tube, which can cause a blowout. An easy on-and-off pumping rhythm will usually slow you down fast enough.

With hand brakes you also have to be careful on rainy days because the brake shoes won't grip the wet rims. Ride slowly in the rain, and occasionally squeeze the brakes lightly to wipe the rims.

It is a good idea to practice sudden braking for an emergency. When you stop a bike quickly, it will tend to pitch forward and throw you over the handlebars. To overcome this, shift your weight to the rear as you brake.

Of course, keep your brakes in good working condition (see p. 22). And if you have hand brakes, position the levers where you can reach them easily and quickly.

Riding Position

A good riding position is essential to a good riding style. But your riding positions will be limited by the kind of handlebars your bike has. If it has conventional raised handlebars, you will ride in a more or less upright position. Most of your weight will be on the seat and the muscles of your legs will do most of the work of pedaling. This is not very efficient, and the more upright you sit the less efficient it is. For casual riding and short trips, this doesn't matter much, but for trips of any distance at all or for going over rough roads, if you lean forward and put some of your weight on the handlebars, you will find it easier to pedal and control the bike. As you lean forward, you are distributing your weight more equally over the bike, which makes it easier to balance and keep going straight, and you are bringing the muscles of the lower trunk into use, making it easier to pedal. You will find leaning forward most comfortable—and you will have better control—if your arms are bent slightly.

With dropped handlebars, you have no choice but to ride leaning forward—more forward than any position you can assume with raised handlebars—which means that you will always be distributing your weight on the bike and using more than your leg muscles. You may find riding forward awkward at first, especially if you assume that you should put your hands on the ends of the handlebars. Actually, this is only one of the riding positions that you can use with dropped handlebars, and it is the least commonly used. Dropped handlebars are usually taped for most of their length; this is done so you can grip them at any point. Where you grip them affects your position. And as you change the location of your hands, you change the number of trunk muscles used and the weight on the handlebars. You also change the angle of the wrist and the part of the hand that the weight is on.

On most dropped handlebars, you can assume four positions. None are exact positions, so put your hands where they feel most comfortable. Vary your positions regularly to avoid tiring yourself.

1 The hands are on the top of the bars close to the stem, and much of the weight is on the seat. This is a coasting or resting position, and many riders use it for long steady riding or for getting the most push out of a tail wind.

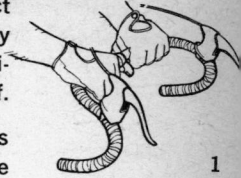

2 The hands are on the top of the forward bend, the rider is at a 45° angle and more weight is on the bars. Most riders use this as their normal riding position.

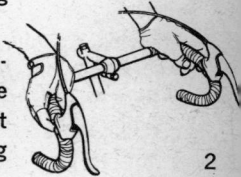

3 The hands are all of the way forward with the base of the brake lever between the thumb and forefinger. It is a strong, efficient position for gaining speed on the level, for most of the trunk muscles are in use. If you feel too far forward like this, move the brake levers.

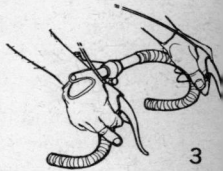

4 The hands are on the lower part of the bars and the body is very far forward, and it should form a relaxed arching C to bring all of the trunk muscles into play. Most riders reserve this position for when they need greater power, balance, or control—as when they are going up a steep hill, cutting through a strong head wind, or negotiating rough terrain. It can also be used, as racing cyclists use it, for gaining speed.

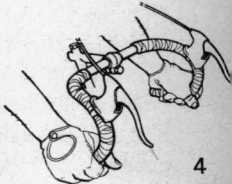

Pedaling

The pedals are where most of your effort is concentrated, so pedaling well is at the heart of a good riding style. And the efficiency of your pedaling will be affected by three things: how you put your feet on the pedals, how you turn them, and the rate at which you turn them.

First, just putting the ball of your foot on the pedals, rather than the instep, will do a great deal to improve the ease and efficiency of your pedaling. With the instep on the pedal you are only using the thigh muscles, but with the ball of the foot, you are using both the calf and thigh muscles. Keeping the ball of the foot on the pedal is not easy when you are going uphill, especially if your bike has rubber pedals. If you live in a hilly area, get metal rattrap pedals with a good grip. Many cyclists use toe clips and straps to keep their feet in position, but you should only use them after you have learned to ride well enough to lean over and unstrap them. Never use them in traffic.

With your feet in the correct position, you will have much less of a tendency to stamp the pedals up and down and should find it easy to learn to press the pedals around in a circular motion. It is important that this be a smooth, continuous, even movement and not an alternate up-and-down pumping. Until you have learned to do this and it is as natural as walking, don't try to learn any more advanced technique of turning the pedals.

Then, you may want to learn "ankling," which is a very efficient way of turning the pedals. In ankling, as the pedal reaches the 6 o'clock, straight-down position, the foot is bent down to bring the pedal as far around as possible. As the foot is carried up, it is quickly bent up and pressure is applied to the pedal well before the 12 o'clock position. In this way, one foot is taking over before the other is finished, and the effort of the legs is overlapping. Ankling is most useful on long steep climbs.

Far more important than any specialized pedaling technique is how often and how regularly you turn the pedals. Your body works most efficiently at a steady, rhythmic pace that is neither too fast nor too slow. A good hiker, for example, has an easy, regular, but quick walk that he can maintain all day. The key to long-distance running is in the pace of the runner. This is just as true for cycling as it is for walking or running—with the added factor of momentum. Up to a point, it is easier to pedal a bike that is going fast than one going slow.

One of your major aims should be to develop a steady, relatively fast pedaling rhythm that feels natural to you. This rhythm will vary depending on the physical condition of the rider and the weight, road resistance, and gears of the bike. On most bikes for most people, this is a cadence of 60 pedal turns a minute—one every second. On a lightweight, it will be faster, up to 80 pedal turns a minute—even more for riders in good condition. This may seem fast at first, but remember that pedaling too slowly is as devitalizing as riding too fast is exhausting. If you need to go slower at first, don't worry; your rhythm will change as the muscles you use for riding become stronger. Your pace should always feel comfortable to you.

Most adult bikes have gears, and the gears should be used to help you keep your natural pedaling cadence. On 3-speeds, you will have to vary your regular pace to get over hills by building up momentum as you approach and pedaling harder as you go up (see p. 63). But on a derailleur, you should have a gear that will let you keep your pace on all but the steepest hills (see p. 49).

On a long trip, however, it does help to vary your rhythm occasionally to keep from getting stale. And you will naturally sprint or coast when you need a momentary change of pace.

Steering

Steering well is primarily a matter of learning to ride as straight as possible. It is important for both efficiency and safety, and essential if you ride in traffic. A forward-leaning position, a relaxed firm grip, and a good momentum all help, but it does take practice, especially on a lightweight. A general guideline is that a rider should be able to keep the wheel within a four-inch path. For best control keep both hands on the handlebars, but learn to steer with one for giving hand signals and changing gears.

Making sharp turns is dangerous. Always slow down for turns and avoid turning the handlebars abruptly. Sharp turns when unavoidable are made by a combination of steering and leaning.

If you look ahead you should have time to avoid potholes, stones, gravel patches, oil or water slicks, pavement breaks, sewer grates, wet leaves, and broken glass. But if you do find yourself on a rough or slippery surface, keep good control over your bike and ride straight through it. If you try to turn or brake, you can fall.

Getting On and Off

Even though you can ride well, you may have trouble getting on and off your bike. The best way to get on is to straddle the frame and grasp the handlebars. Bring one pedal around to the one o'clock position and put your foot on it. Then simultaneously push down on the pedal, push yourself off the ground with the other foot, and lift yourself onto the seat. If you do it properly, you'll find that you are going forward with enough momentum that you can easily get your other foot on the pedal.

To stop and get off, first slow your bike down by coasting or braking gently. Then, keeping one foot on the lower pedal, slide forward off the seat while extending your other foot to the ground and applying the brakes.

Safety

Good riding technique will naturally make you a much safer rider. You will have better control of your bike, and you are less likely to tire yourself to the point where you can't ride alertly. But if you have to, always be ready to compromise on technique for safety. In traffic, the best position for your hand is on the brake levers and the best pace is a slow one. The same is true at night.

Bicycles are subject to the same traffic laws as cars and often even more since they are considered slow moving vehicles. But they all come down to two rules:

Keep to the right of the road. This means riding with the flow of traffic and along the side of the road, not out in the traffic lanes. It may seem dangerous to have cars coming behind you but it is much safer than having them come head on, even though you can't see them. Since you are moving in the same direction as the car, even if the driver doesn't see you until he is practically on top of you he still has time enough and room enough to avoid you. And if you do get hit, the impact will be less severe than in a head-on collision. Also, neither drivers nor pedestrians will be looking for you coming from an unexpected direction. The only exception to this rule is on one-way streets with buses in the right lane. Then, it is safer to ride on the left. It follows from this rule that two or more bikes should ride single file—always with enough space between to brake.

Be careful at intersections: Stop for red lights. At stopsign-controlled intersections, stop even if you have the right of way. As you approach, use hand signals to let cars know what you plan to do. Bending your left arm up means you are going to make a right turn, bending it down means you are going to stop, and extending it straight out means you are going to turn left.

Seats

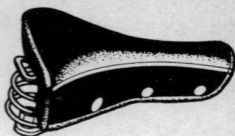

MATTRESS

Seats, or saddles as they are still called, come in a variety of sizes and shapes and vary greatly in quality and comfort. But there are only three basic types made for adult bikes:* the wide mattress-spring seat, the narrow springless racing seat, and the loop-spring seat, which is in-between.

The mattress seat has two large rear springs that absorb the body weight and give the rider a cushioned ride. It is intended to be used with the nearly upright position that most people assume when they ride. For most casual riding, especially short rides around the neighborhood or the park, this seat is fine, although many people find that the width of this seat causes soreness and chafing during longer rides. Most of these seats are covered with a plastic of poor quality, and if you have to replace yours after a couple of years, you'll be better off getting one made of leather or a good quality plastic.

The racing seat is preferred by most cyclists who ride a lot for both efficiency and comfort. But most of these cyclists ride in a forward position with part of their weight on dropped handlebars, and the racing seat is designed for this riding position. For efficiency, the seat doesn't have springs so that none of the pedaling effort is absorbed in the springs. But since there is less weight on it, it is still possible to be comfortable on the springless seat. The seat is narrow because a wider one would limit the movement of the thighs. Racing seats are avail-

* For the banana seat used children's bikes, see p. 35.

RACING

LOOP-SPRING

able in many shapes and makes, and they are usually covered with plastic or one of many grades of leather.

The loop-spring seat is a compromise between the other two types. Although it could be classified as a racing seat, it usually comes on the best quality 3-speed English bikes. Like a racing seat, it doesn't have the large rear mattress springs, and like good ones, it is usually covered with leather. But it is much wider than most racing seats—almost as wide as a conventional seat—and the supporting wires underneath the seat are looped at the rear to give it some springiness. Although expensive, it is a good compromise that is preferred by many riders.

Leather or plastic is used to cover seats. The plastic seats, which require little care and don't have to be broken in, are fine for ordinary riding. But on a hot day or on long rides, they can get very sticky. Leather seats are usually better quality and longer lasting, but it takes a few weeks to break one in, and long rides or tours with a new one are likely to leave you sore. Many people who tour work neet's foot oil or Vaseline into the underside of the leather to soften it. Leather seats also need to be saddle soaped occasionally to preserve the leather. And as they get older, they tend to sag, but they can be tightened by turning the nut under the nose of the seat.

If you have a leather seat or any seat with padding, take along a plastic bag with a rubber band or an old shower cap to cover it on rainy days. This not only prolongs the life of the seat but saves you a wet ride home.

Seat Height and Position

The height of the seat of your bike affects the efficiency of your pedaling. Up to a point, the more fully your leg is extended when you are pedaling, the more efficiently you use your leg muscles. The usual rule is that the seat should be high enough so that your leg is fully extended when you are seated and your heel is on the down pedal. That way, when you move your foot to the recommended riding position with the ball of the foot on the pedal, your knee will be slightly bent giving you just enough flexibility to turn the pedals smoothly, to absorb bumps, and to get on and off easily. This height is good if you are going for long, uninterrupted distances as, for example, when you are touring. At the end of a day, it can mean the difference between being pleasantly tired or completely exhausted. But if you usually ride for short distances or in traffic where you stop frequently, you will be better off with a less efficient, but safer position a few inches lower.

If you can't move your bike seat high or low enough, you may have a bike with the wrong frame size for you (see p. 7). If the frame is too small, you can get a longer seat post (get the right diameter). But it is not safe to ride a bike with a frame that is too large for you.

The horizontal (back and forth) position can also be adjusted on most seats. The recommended position is with the nose of the seat about 2 inches behind the center of the pedal crank. This position allows the most effective use of the leg muscles when you are riding at moderate speeds. But if you usually ride fast, the best position is further forward.

The tilt of a seat can also be adjusted to fit the rider. There is no rule on this but comfort. And most riders are comfortable when the seat is level or when the nose is tilted up slightly.

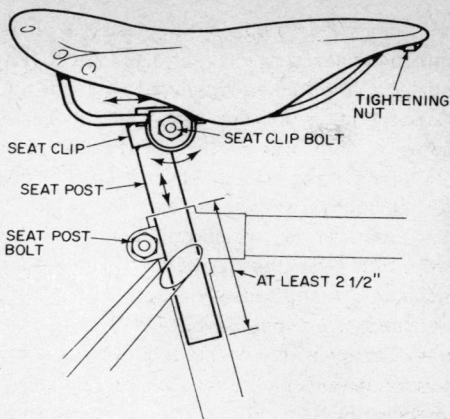

To adjust height: Loosen seat-post bolt and move seat post up or down by working the seat side to side. There should be at least 2½ inches of post left in the seat tube. Check straightness before retightening.

To make a seat even lower: Invert the brackets of the seat clip so that they point downward. This involves removing the seat-clip bolt, inverting the brackets, and reassembling.

To move forward or backward: Loosen seat-clip bolt and slide seat along bars or wires. Check tilt and straightness before retightening bolt. If your seat can't be adjusted horizontally, you can remove the seat and reverse the direction of the seat clip.

To adjust tilt: Loosen seat-clip bolt and rotate seat up or down. Retighten bolt.

To replace seat: Loosen seat-clip bolt and pull the old seat straight up to remove. Put the clip of new seat on the post, check tilt and straightness, and tighten bolt.

To correct wobbly seat: Check seat-clip bolt and seat-post bolt and tighten either or both.

To tighten sagging leather seat: Tighten the small nut under the nose of the seat.

Tires

A tire is designed to fit a particular type of bicycle, taking into consideration the performance that will be expected from that bike. When stability and comfort are most important, as on middleweights, children's, and folding bikes, a wide low-pressure tire, which grips the road and cushions bumps is used. But on bikes where it is most important to gain speed with the least effort, a narrow low-pressure tire, which minimizes road resistance is used. And on other bikes, such as English 3-speeds, the tire used is a compromise between these two extremes.

There are two types of bicycle tires, but most bikes come equipped with the kind known as "wired-on" or "clincher" tires, which are scaled-down versions of the automobile tire. These tires are called wired-ons because they have wires inside the edge (or "bead") of the casing which hold the tire firmly on the rim. Getting the wired edges off and on the rim is the most difficult part of changing a tire. Clincher tires are also known as "tube" tires since they have separate inner tubes, but this name can easily be confused with the name of the other type of tire, the "tubular" tire. Tubulars are the light racing tires with the tube sewn in an unwired casing. Since their use is limited to expensive lightweights and they are not interchangeable with conventional tires, they are covered separately on p. 121. Even on lightweights, the conventional wired-on tires are preferable for ordinary use because they are more durable and easier to repair.

Nearly all wired-on tires are made of synthetic rubber, have nylon cords, and come with a utilitarian tread suitable for general purpose riding. A typical tire might have parallel center treads for smooth straight riding and zigzag side treads to give you more grip on turns. Although not always easy to find at your local bike shop, a variety of other tread patterns are made, ranging from almost smooth for riding on obstacle-free paved surfaces to

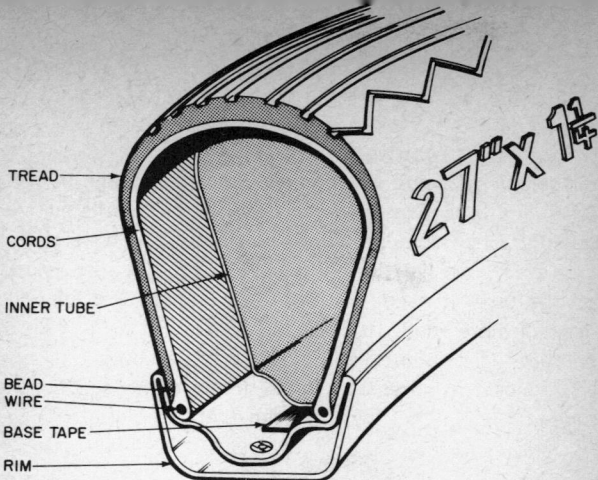

TREAD
CORDS
INNER TUBE
BEAD
WIRE
BASE TAPE
RIM

27" x 1¼

knobby, tractor-like treads for riding on rough surfaces. But these special patterns are not available in all sizes.

If you have a 3-speed or single-speed bike, you will probably settle for the tire that your bike shop stocks and find it satisfactory. But if you have a lightweight, you should be more selective. Since so little tire surface is in contact with the road, the tread is very important and should suit the kind of riding you do. And, since so much stress is put on a narrow, high-pressure tire, you should consider "gum-wall" tires, which have sidewalls made of a yellowish, translucent rubber to withstand the extra flexing there.

The size of a tire is embossed on its sidewall. It appears as a figure, such as $26'' \times 1\frac{3}{8}''$. The first number is the diameter of the tire, which is usually called the wheel size, and the second number is its width. The same figures are stamped on the inner tube. A tire or inner tube has to be replaced with one of the same size.

Most of the damage to tires comes from running over potholes, stones, and glass, and they should be avoided whenever possible. You should also avoid jumping curbs, which will break the tire cords, and skidding, which will wear out the treads.

Maintenance and Repair

Proper air pressure will prevent a lot of damage to your tires. All tires lose air and need to be reinflated frequently. They should be checked every few days if you ride every day. If a tire flattens when you put your weight on the bike, it needs air. An underinflated tire not only creates more road drag but is much more vulnerable to ruptures from bumps and is likely to be cut by the rim.

The best air pressure for a tire is embossed on the sidewall. The usual figures given are:

Bike	Tire size	Air pressure
Derailleurs	27" × 1¼"	70–75+ lbs per sq. in.
3-speeds	26" × 1⅜"	55–60 lbs per sq. in.
Middleweights	26" × 1¾"	40–45 lbs per sq. in.
Childrens; folding	20" × 2.125"	25–35 lbs per sq. in.

These are for bikes with riders of average weight without a heavy load. If you weigh more or are carrying a full load, you may need more air. On hot days, you will need less, because the air in the tire will expand.

Be careful not to put too much air in your tires. An overinflated tire will blow out very quickly. The safest way to fill a tire is with a manual pump, and a foot pump that you keep at home is much easier to use than a hand pump which clips to your bike. If you use the air pump in a filling station, you have to be extra careful because car tires take much more pressure than bike tires. On these pumps, the air comes in high-pressure pulses and even if you can dial the air pressure, it only takes a few seconds to fill a bike tire. The best way to test air pressure is with a small pen-shaped air gauge, which will more than pay for itself in averted blowouts. If you don't have one, the only test is to squeeze the tire. If it still has some give and doesn't flatten when you get on the bike, the tire is properly inflated.

The procedures for repairing tires are given on the following pages. The most common tire problems are:

Slow leaks are often caused by faulty valve stems, and they can usually be fixed without changing the tire (see p. 120). Slow leaks also develop in old tubes and they should be replaced.

Simple punctures can often be patched without removing the wheel if you know where the puncture is. You can often find it by filling the tire and listening for a hiss. If you can't find it, you'll have to remove the wheel, and at that point, it's recommended that you replace the tube. A new tube is safer than a patched tube.

Blowouts, serious punctures, and cracked valve stems, will require you to remove the wheel and replace the inner tube. If the casing is also damaged, replace it.

Worn or damaged tires should be replaced as soon as possible. Check your tires regularly for wear, damage, and embedded materials that might cause a flat.

Old tires discolor and crack after five or six years—or less if the bike is not stored properly. They should be replaced before trouble develops while you are riding.

Tools should be used with care on tires since there is a good chance you will pinch the tube or rip the edge of the casing if you are not careful. A sharp tool such as a screwdriver should never be used to pry off a tire. Low-pressure tires can usually be removed by hand, but to remove higher pressure tires, you'll probably need two or three tire irons. These are the small bicycle tire irons, which can be hooked on the spokes as you pry off the tire (see next page). Although most inner tubes now come with plastic valve caps, the older metal valve caps are very handy. Inverted, they can be used to tighten leaky valves and to deflate the tires.

Changing a Tire

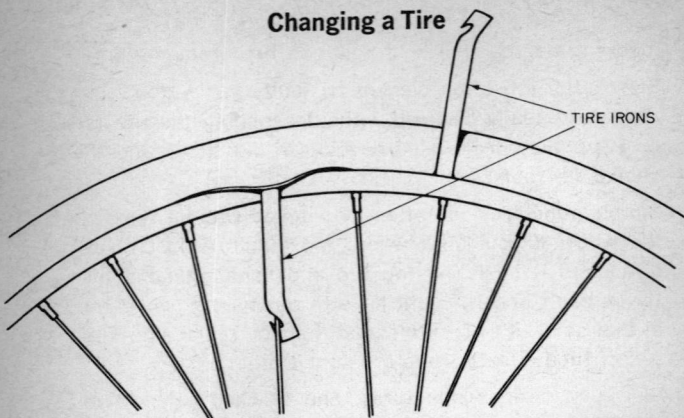

TIRE IRONS

To remove a tire: Put your bike upside down, on a rack, or on its left (non-chain) side resting on a piece of cardboard. If tire is not completely flat, deflate it (see p. 120).

1 Remove the wheel. If it is the front wheel, simply loosen the axle nuts. If it is the back wheel, see the procedure on p. 135.

2 Loosen the tire from the rim by squeezing it all around. If you have a metal valve stem, remove the nut that holds it on.

3 At the end opposite to the valve, grab the tire and roll it to one side until you can get a finger or tire iron under the edge of the casing.

4 With the tire irons or your fingers, carefully pry the edge of the casing over the rim. If you are using tire irons, you can hook them to the spokes as you move around, but once you can get your fingers under the edge of the tire, use them and work your way around the tire until one edge of the casing is completely free.

At this point, you can take out the inner tube without removing the rest of the tire. Although it is easy to work the other edge of the tire off the rim, it's best not to, if you are only changing the tube, since it is difficult to get back on.

If you want to patch your tube instead of replacing it, turn over the page. If you replace the tube or the tire, be sure to get the right size.

To replace a tire: Before you do, check the tire for embedded glass and tacks and the rim for rough spoke ends that can cause a puncture. If necessary, remove the tire completely and the protective base tape around the rim, and file down the spoke ends. Be sure to replace the base tape.

1 If you took the tire completely off, work one edge of the casing around the rim. Getting the last bit back on will be difficult; if you have to use a tire iron, be careful not to tear the edge of the tire.

2 Inflate the tube just enough to give it a shape. Putting some talcum powder on the tube will help to keep it from catching inside the tire.

3 Tuck the tube carefully into the tire, starting by inserting the valve stem in the hole in the rim. Put on the valve stem nut if you have one.

4 Starting at the valve stem end, work the other edge of the tire onto the rim. Be sure that you keep the tube well inside the tire and the valve stem straight as you work your way around the tire. Again, getting the last bit on will be difficult, and if you have to use a tire iron be very careful not to pinch the tube or tear the edge of the tire.

5 To keep the tube from kinking, inflate it a little more and bounce the tire as you turn it and squeeze it. Then, deflate the tube so that it can resettle.

6 Inflate the tube to full pressure and check for leaks. Make sure the valve stem is straight.

You are ready to remount the wheel. If you have trouble getting the tire past the rim brake unit and you don't have quick-release brakes, letting some air out will help. If it is a back wheel, you will have to adjust the chain tension and may have to reconnect and adjust the hub gears or re-attach the arm of the coaster brakes (see p. 135). On bikes with rim brakes, be sure to check the position of the brake shoes.

Valves

To deflate a tire: Press down the pin-head valve core in the top of the valve stem. Use an inverted metal valve top or the edge of a screwdriver.

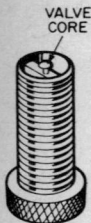

VALVE
CORE

To fix a leaky valve: First, test it by refilling the tire, putting some water or spit on the tip of your finger, and rubbing it lightly over the top of the stem. If it bubbles, tighten the valve by inserting an inverted metal valve cap in the top of the stem and gently turning clockwise. Try this a couple of times. If it doesn't work, you can replace the valve core by screwing the old valve core out counterclockwise and screwing a new one in.

Patching

To patch without removing wheel when you only have a simple puncture and you know where it is: Follow procedure for removing and replacing tire on previous pages, working only in the area of the puncture and prying the tire open just enough to get a foot or so of the tube out. Patch as described below.

To find a tube leak: Remove the tube and fill it to more than its normal pressure. If you can't hear the leak hissing, slowly rotate it through a tub of water until bubbles appear. Mark area with chalk so you can find it.

To patch a tube using a standard patch kit:

1 Clean the area of the tube with puncture; make sure it is dry before you go on.

2 Roughen the area with sandpaper or scraper-top of kit.

3 Cover the area with rubber cement. Be sure there is enough for the patch. Let it get tacky.

4 Pull the backing off the patch. Be careful not to touch the sticky side.

5 Press the patch firmly in place, make sure it is smooth, and let it dry. Remove excess cement.

Tubular Tires

Tubular, or "sew-up" tires were developed for racing and track bikes. They are small, weighing only 5–16 ounces. They have a circular cross-section with the tube sewn up in the casing, and both the tire and tube are much thinner than on conventional tires. They fit in special shallow rims and are held on by glue or double-stick tape.

For racing, they have advantages in addition to their light weight: a minimum of tire surface is in contact with the road; a folded spare can be carried under the seat; changes are fast and easy; and a wide range of special cords and treads are available. But for ordinary riding, these advantages are outweighed by their cost, their greater vulnerability to puncture, and their lesser stability. And although they are easy to change, they are difficult to repair—or expensive to get repaired. In spite of these problems, many riders prefer them—finding them more responsive. If you have sew-ups or plan to get a bike with them, here are some hints: Stick to the heavier, "training" weight tires, which weigh around 16 ounces. Check the air in them every day; the thin tube under high-pressure loses air by osmosis. They have a special valve stem, a Presta stem, and unless you have a hand pump for this stem, you will need an adapter. Inflate your spares regularly, leave them overnight, and refold them to avoid having the folds "set" and ruin the tire. Old spares are dangerous on a long trip. When you put on a tubular tire, you can either use rubber cement, a coat on the tire and one or two coats on the rim, or a special double-stick tape. The tape saves time but won't always hold at high speeds or with a heavy load. To repair a sew-up, you have to find the puncture, undo the stitching in the area, pull out the tube in the area, patch it, and restitch the tire in the same holes. A special kit with thin patches is needed.

Touring

Traveling by bike is an art. But if you plan your trip carefully, select your equipment prudently, and use good riding technique, you will be well on your way to mastering it. You don't have to have a rigid plan, expensive equipment, or perfect technique, but you can't just hop on a bike and go. If you do, you may find it a laborious nightmare rather than an exhilarating adventure.

Planning

The best time of year to tour is the spring or fall. The cooler temperatures are better suited to active cycling than the heat of summer, and you also avoid the clogged roads and crowded campgrounds that go with it.

How far you go each day will depend mostly on your physical condition, although it will also be affected by the kind of bike you ride, the terrain you cover, and the load you carry. You will also want to have time and energy for other activities. Some people start with as little as 10 or 20 miles a day, and many experienced riders—"century" riders—cover 100 miles a day. The important thing is to enjoy yourself. Cycling shouldn't be hard work—unless that's what you enjoy.

To make it enjoyable, get into condition before you tour. Ride every day and build up your capacity gradually. Try some day excursions—exploring another part of town or a nearby countryside. Start touring with short overnight trips. Don't jump headlong into a three-week tour.

Planning a route that avoids heavy traffic and rough and hilly roads can mean the difference between continuing to tour or giving up after the first day. For deciding the general area where you want to travel, you can use an auto road map. But these maps are highway maps, and you should make a rule of avoiding highways—federal or state—if it is at all possible. Instead, you should look for a more indirect route over local roads that are relatively free of traffic, but still well paved. To find them, you will need detailed local maps. One good way to get these maps is to find the county seats of the counties that you'll be passing through and write to the county engineer in each for a map. With them, you can usually find older, well-kept roads, often running parallel to highways and now bypassed by most cars, which not only take you where you want to go but give you much better views. If the area is at all hilly, you may want to get a topological map of the area from the U.S. Geological Survey. These maps are generally too large for road use, but they are good for planning a route around—not over—hills.

Where you stay overnight will depend on your preferences and budget. If you like camping, cycle touring can be combined with it. If you can afford them and want to keep your load light, you can stay in hotels, motels, or rooming houses and eat in restaurants. If you don't like camping, can't afford motels, and don't mind dormitory-style accommodations and rules, you can join American Youth Hostels, no matter what your age is, and stay in their hostels—provided you are traveling in an area where they are well established (such as in the Eastern U.S.). Or, you can combine motels, camping, and hostels.

For information on campgrounds, there are several campground atlases published and updated annually. But information on them, hotels, motels, rooming houses— and local sights and recreational facilities—can usually be obtained from state departments of commerce and tourism or local chambers of commerce. And if the nearest large city doesn't have a local American Youth Hostels office, you can write their national headquarters (20 W. 17 St., New York, N.Y. 10011). They are also a good source for touring equipment and organize group tours.

Riding

Good riding technique is essential if you are to avoid exhausting yourself when you are riding for long uninterrupted distances. In general, the best riding position is a forward-leaning one with the hands along the top of the dropped handlebars, and the best pace is achieved with relatively fast pedaling in a lower than normal gear. The suggestions in the chapter, "Riding Techniques," pp. 102–9, are especially relevant to touring. And wind, hills, and load will require using gears to your advantage (see p. 49). Remember that an experienced rider uses half the energy an inexperienced rider does.

Riding in the country—which is what you will probably be doing most of the time you are touring—is different than riding around the neighborhood or in the city. In the first place, it's likely to be much more pleasant. You can go for miles without seeing more than two or three cars. Since there are fewer cars, you may be inclined to forget about them. But you have to be as alert as always, because rural drivers often assume that the road is theirs and unless they can see or hear another vehicle, they are very likely to drive as fast as they want and to use any part of the road. Although you will usually be able to hear a car coming on a quiet country road, it is not safe to make a habit of riding out in the road. It is safest to ride on the far right side of the road—just far enough into the road so that you won't stray off the shoulder if you are distracted. The most danger for you as a cyclist is when the driver of a car approaching behind you can't see you —just after you have rounded a sharp curve or gone over the crest of a steep hill. On a sharp right turn, the driver is likely to be hugging the side of the road, and in this case, it is usually safer for you to move over to the far left side of the road—temporarily. As always, the best policy is to give any car the right of way at an intersection. Rural drivers also tend to ignore stop signs.

On country roads you should be able to veer around most obstacles if you watch the road, but be ready to handle unbalancing surfaces by leaning forward, keeping firm but relaxed control of your bike, and driving straight through them. Making turns or braking is dangerous. And although it is best to avoid them, use the same technique on sandy, pebbly, or rut-filled dirt roads.

Dogs, who run loose in rural areas, are another hazard that you should be prepared to handle. Sometimes, they can be very dangerous. Depending on how threatening the dog really is, you can choose any of these common methods of handling one: shooing it away, outrunning it, getting off and walking with the bike between you and the dog, and repelling it with a switch or a chemical spray— either the commercial ones used by postmen or slightly watered ammonia in a squirt gun.

Riding with a load will affect both your balance and pace, and a fully loaded bike will be difficult to handle until you get use to it. Either learn to ride with extra weight before you tour or take it easy for the first couple of days. In addition to using lower gears to compensate for the load, you can make it easier if you keep the load low on the bike and balanced side to side and front to back.

A good rule for touring is to take care of your needs before they become necessities. Change your hand position before your arms hurt. Rest before you're exhausted. Put on more clothing before you're chilled. Take some off before you're hot. Eat before you're starving. Drink before you're parched. And go to the bathroom before you have to. It's not only healthier, but safer. You can keep your attention on the road and not on personal needs.

Equipment

If you multiply every pound you pull by every pedal turn you will make on a tour, you'll get a good idea of the importance of lightweight equipment. But—in buying a bike and camping equipment—you pay a premium for every pound you don't pedal. If you carry a full camping load, try to keep it under 40 pounds—not counting the bike. If you travel in groups, share equipment to save weight.

Bicycle: The best is a 10-speed derailleur that weighs less than 30 pounds. The less expensive 10-speeds offer the same flexibility in gearing and the 5-speeds the same range without flexibility, but you'll be carrying an extra ten pounds. Three-speeds, which give you the extra ten pounds without gear range or flexibility, were used for touring for years and still can be if you are in condition and limit your mileage, load, and terrain. If you travel in mountainous areas, you'll need a 15-speed with the lowest gear in the low 30's. For more on bikes, see p. 6.

Whichever bike you use, check it thoroughly a few days before you go. You'll then have time to fix anything that is loose, frayed, or worn. Use pp. 88–93 as a guide.

Here are some recommendations on specific parts:

Handlebars: Dropped are best, either Maes or Randonneur.

Seat: A narrow racing seat covered with leather is recommended, but it should be broken in first for several weeks. Vaseline or neet's foot oil worked in with a rolling pin helps.

Gears: On derailleurs, you need a freewheel that gives you a wide range of gears. On a 3-speed, you may want to consider lowering your gears or adding a derailleur (see p. 64).

Tires: Although tubulars have their advocates, clincher tires are usually better for touring.

Fenders: Add them. Full wide ones will keep a lot of dust, mud, and water off you and your bags.

Pedals: Metal rattraps give a better grip. And toe clips and straps are useful in hilly country.

Touring bags: Expensive, lightweight nylon bags are best, but you can get along fine with the less-expensive, heavier ones made of vinyl cloth. And if you can attach them securely to your bike, canvas army-surplus bags can be adapted by inserting stiff cardboard as backing. Backpacks are not recommended for bike tours. They put a tiring load on your shoulders, limit body movement, and make you top heavy.

1 Pannier bags carry the load low and are essential for long tours. They fit over a metal carrier and attach to the chain stays. Smaller front panniers can be used also, and for a heavy load they are better than handlebar or seat bags.

2 A handlebar bag can be used for overnight trips or as an auxiliary "day" bag on long trips. Many have a plastic window on top for maps. Look for one that you can open without dismounting. A metal support is usually needed.

3 A seat-attached touring bag (a large roomy one) can be used for overnight trips, but for longer trips panniers are better. The smaller seat bags can be used for tools.

In packing, if you always put things in, in the same order, you can find what you want quickly. To keep the load low, pack heavy objects at the bottom of each pannier.

Bike repair kit: Here is a suggested list for longer trips. For more details on tools, see p. 86.

Tools	Spare parts
screwdriver	inner tube
crescent wrench (6-inch)	or tubular tires (2)
or metric wrench set	valve core
or bike spanner	brake shoes (2)
pump	front axle nut
tire irons (2)	rear axle nut
patch kit	master link (3-speed)
spoke wrench	indicator rod (3-speed)
light oil (seal tightly)	spokes (fit in pump)
chain rivet tool (derailleur)	back brake cable wire

Clothing: This is up to you. On overnight trips you only need a change of underwear and socks. But on longer trips, you'll need a change of outer clothes, too. Depending on the season, you should take something like this, including what you are wearing:

Basic	Warm weather	Cool weather
pants or jeans	shorts	extra pants
long-sleeved shirt	short-sleeved shirt	wool shirt
underwear	extra underwear	extra underwear
socks	extra socks	heavy socks
windbreaker	swimming suit	sweater

Shoes should be low cut, flexible, and comfortable. There is more on shoes on p. 40, along with information on rain and safety wear and other clothing suggestions. You may also need a hat for sun or cold. Remember, light and bright clothing will be seen faster by a motorist.

Miscellaneous: Take first-aid kit, soap, small towel, and toiletries. If hosteling, a sleeping sack.

Water: Water for the road can be carried in a caged water bottle attached to the frame. Additional ones are good for other liquids.

Food: If you are hosteling or camping, buy food late in the day—getting enough for a filling dinner, a light high-protein breakfast, and a small picnic lunch on the road. The idea is never to ride with a full stomach. Certain staples that you can't purchase in small quantities can be taken in tightly sealed plastic containers or bags, such as salt, pepper, sugar, cooking oil, instant coffee, tea bags, rice, noodles, oatmeal, and flour. The hiker's powdered and freeze-dried foods are not useful to most cyclists who are mobile enough to buy food as they go. Most nested cooking kits contain all the pots, pans, dishes, and cups you'll need. But if you are camping, the stove you get may come with pots. For cooking and eating, you also need a knife, fork, and spoon, both kinds of can openers, and matches in a waterproof container. And for cleaning up, you need scouring pads and a small dish towel.

Camping equipment: The lightest is sold in stores that specialize in backpacking equipment. You'll need:

Tent: A lightweight, expensive nylon one is best, but an inexpensive tube tent is light and will do if you bring poles and a rope and don't mind bugs. Also, shelters can be made from tarps in warm dry weather.

Sleeping bag: A lightweight down one is best in cool weather, but a cheaper one will do in summer. An air mattress can be taken for comfort, but it adds weight.

Stove: Small compact liquid-fuel ones are best. But Sterno stoves work. Don't carry too much extra fuel. Buy it along the way. Be sure to keep fuel away from food.

Other: A small ax or folding saw, a good combination pocket-knife, a lantern, a fold-up water container, several plastic bags and rubber bands, heavy cord, metal mirror, toilet paper, and insect repellant.

If the tent and sleeping bag won't fit in your bags, they can be strapped on top of the rear carrier.

Transporting a Bike

By Plane, Train, or Bus

Whether or not you can take your bike with you on a long trip by train, bus, or plane will depend on the carrier company's policy. Most take bikes—occasionally as baggage at no extra cost, but usually for an additional-baggage charge. Most airlines require that bikes be boxed; most buses and trains—depending on how much other baggage they have and the mood of the ticket clerk—will accept a bike rolled up to the counter. Call in advance to find out what the policy is. Many cyclists find that they are usually successful when they just appear with their bikes; but allow time for the arrangements.

Although it is not convenient, you may want to box your bike even if the carrier doesn't require it to prevent damage—especially if you have a lightweight with bendable alloy and other expensive-to-replace parts. Some airlines supply boxes, but in most cases you have to get your own. The best source is a local bike shop—where, in addition, you might be able to see how a new bike is packed as a guide to packing yours. Usually you will have to remove the seat, pedals, and front wheel—which should only take a few minutes. You may also have to remove the handlebars, but first try to get them in by turning them sideways and adjusting the angle. If you do remove them, be careful not to kink the cables. You can put a small piece of wood in the fork as spacer to keep it from being bent. Avoid getting a box so small that you have to also take off the back wheel.

When carrying a bike by plane, partially deflate the tires so they won't blow out in the low-pressure hold.

Unless you have a folding bike, your bike will probably not be allowed on local public transportation, although it may be permitted on some commuter trains, especially during non-rush hours. Nearly all ferries permit bikes for a small fee.

By Car

If you remove the front wheels, you can carry two bikes in the trunk of most cars. But if you have other luggage or a small trunk, you'll need a bike carrier. Here are the basic types:

Bumper carriers have two vertical supports with hangers and straps for your bikes. They can be adjusted to clamp onto most rear bumpers, but some need a piece of wood as backing. They will hold two bikes—or up to four if you remove the front wheels and run guy lines to the top of the trunk for support. These carriers are easy to get to, but limit access to the trunk and, in addition, the bikes can collect a lot of road dirt and grit. On a car with low road clearance, mount the carrier as high as you can and avoid sudden drops and steep driveways. On all cars, be careful when you're backing up; the bikes are held in a very vulnerable position.

Roof carrier bars, either the ordinary ones sold in auto supply stores or special ones adapted for bikes, can be used to carry bikes upside down on a car top with the handlebars on one bar and the seat on the other. If you alternate the direction of the bikes, you can get from four to six on. Be sure to pad the bars and attach the bikes securely. You can use rope, luggage straps, old toe straps, or large "rubber bands" cut from old inner tubes. The bars that clamp to the rain gutters of the roof are more secure than the ones with suction cups and hooks. With roof carriers you have to be careful of low overheads—trees, bridges, and garages. Getting the bike on and off is more difficult than it is with a bumper carrier.

Other small carriers, especially designed for bikes, will hold two or three bikes. They fit on the trunk top of large cars or the roof of any car. On the trunk they limit access, but again the bikes are easy to get to.

Wheels

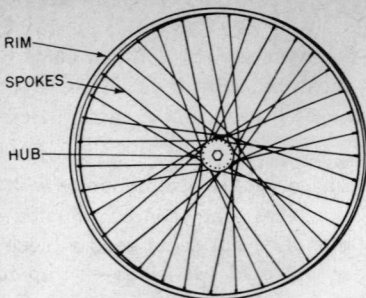

RIM
SPOKES
HUB

The bicycle wheel is an excellent example of good engineering. Held together by the tension of a few dozen wires, it is able to carry more than a hundred times its own weight. It is many times lighter and easier to turn than it would be as a structurally solid unit, although it is much more fragile.

Most wheels are, however, durable—the hubs, rims, and spokes are made of steel, and the spokes are heavy gauge. But they are only as durable as a mass-produced rolling web of stretched wires can be. They will withstand a lot of hard everyday use, but not misuse. The rims are easily bent by jumping curbs and will warp to one side or go out of round if broken or loose spokes are left unattended. The ball bearings in the hubs will go if the hubs don't receive occasional lubrication or if the wheel is not adjusted when it becomes so loose that it wiggles or so hard to turn that it binds. And the unchromed spokes will rust if the bike is habitually left outdoors. But if these utilitarian wheels, which are found on most bikes, are not abused and receive minimal care, they will give many years of use and cover many thousands of miles.

The wheels on better lightweights are an example of the structural engineering of the bike wheel carried to its highest point. By using aluminum alloy for the rims and the hubs and thinner gauge high-tensile steel for the spokes, these wheels are ultralight and are able to carry, relatively, an enormous amount of weight. But although their structural design and more careful manufacture compensates greatly for the inherent weakness of the softer alloy, they are much more fragile than their mass-produced counterparts. They will not withstand as much hard use and will require more care to function well. Although the usually chromed spokes are not likely to rust, the shallow rims are easily bent by a bad bump or pulled out of shape by poorly adjusted spokes. And the precision-made hubs, which are machined from one piece of aluminum alloy, can easily become worn if the bearings are not kept well lubricated and well adjusted. Many of these hubs have high flanges that give the wheel greater structural strength by making the spokes cross over more often. However, these spokes tend to break more often because they are bent more than tangentally.

The size of a wheel is its diameter with the tire on. And the width is the width of the tire it holds. The size is embossed on the side of the tire. On most 26- and 27-inch wheels (which are used on full-size adult bikes) there are 36 spokes—although many imported 3-speeds have 32 in the front and 40 in the rear. Smaller wheels have less spokes. The spokes are usually completely symmetrical, fanning out equally from each side of the hub to the rim. But the rear wheels of derailleurs are "dished"—which means that the spokes on the free-wheel side are three or four turns tighter than the ones on the other side, so that the rim of the wheel will be centered on the frame of the bike to compensate for the space taken up by the freewheel.

On the following pages, the procedures for removing and replacing wheels and for adjusting and replacing spokes are given. A trouble-shooting chart is on p. 137.

Notes

To work on wheels, put your bike upside down, on a rack, or on its left (non-chain) side, resting on a piece of cardboard.

If the wheel turns when you try to loosen one axle nut at a time, use two wrenches and loosen both at the same time. Since both loosen counterclockwise, you will be turning them in opposite directions.

If the rim brake unit blocks the wheel when you are taking it off or putting it on, it is usually easier to deflate the tire slightly than it is to release the brakes—unless your bike has quick-release brakes (see p. 24). Always check the brake shoes' position when you replace the wheel.

If your bike has quick-release hubs, you only have to flip the lever out to release the wheel. When you replace the wheel, close it. The lever goes on the left (non-chain) side. If it doesn't close tightly, re-open lever and tighten the right nut slightly.

Front Wheel

To remove: Loosen both axle nuts and spin them out to the ends of the axle (or off). Lift wheel out of fork.

To replace: First, check cones. If only one has two flated edges, it goes on left (non-chain) side. Then, place wheel in fork, check straightness, and tighten axle nuts.

Fenders

To remove: First, detach supports by removing small bolts in dropout flange (or axle nuts). Then, remove screw or rim brake bolt that holds fender to the frame. If angled clip at this point ever breaks, you can get a replacement at a bike shop.

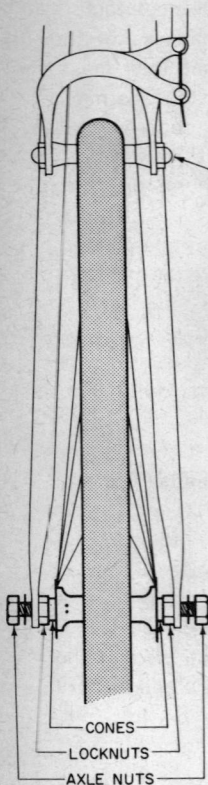

CONES
LOCKNUTS
AXLE NUTS

Back Wheel

With 3-speed hub gears: Before you remove the wheel, disconnect the gear cable and remove the long tubular nut on the right side of the axle (see pp. 66–67). After you replace the wheel, reconnect and readjust the gears. Also, see note on rim brakes on left page.

With derailleur gears: Before removing wheel, shift the chain onto the smallest rear sprocket while turning pedals. When you replace wheel, put the chain back on the smallest sprocket. Also, see notes about releasing rim brakes and quick-release hubs on left page.

With coaster brakes: Before you remove wheel, disconnect the brake arm. After you put the wheel back on, reattach it.

To remove wheel: As for the front wheel, loosen axle nuts and spin them out to the edge of the axle. (If you have carrier supports on the axle, remove axle nuts so you can get the supports off). Push the wheel forward and out of the dropouts. Lift the chain off the sprocket and pull the wheel off. On derailleur bikes, you have to hold the changer back to let the axle by.

To replace wheel: Put the chain back around sprocket. Slide the axle into the dropouts (put on any carrier supports), and tighten the axle nuts by hand. Then, pull the wheel back until the chain has $\frac{1}{2}$-inch play up and down (slightly more on derailleurs). Holding the wheel there, make sure it is centered, tighten the axle nut on the chain side to the bike, and then the one on the other side. This can easily be done by two people—one holds the wheel while the other tightens the nut.

Hubs

If the wheel has too much side play or if it won't turn freely, you can adjust the left cone if you first loosen the axle nut (and the locknut if you have one) and then move the cone in or out a quarter-turn at a time. The full procedure is explained on pp. 95–98. The overhaul and repair of hubs is also covered there. But rear hubs with coaster brakes or hub gears should be adjusted or overhauled by a mechanic only.

Spokes

BASE TAPE

RIM

NIPPLE

TOOL

SPOKE

BRAKE SHOES

TIGHTEN

LOOSEN

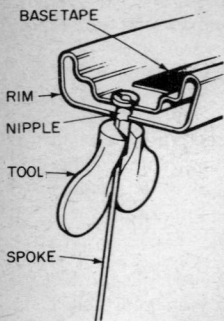

Note: Spokes are screwed into nipples in the rim. The nipples are slotted and can be adjusted with a screwdriver—if you remove the tire. But with a spoke wrench, you can adjust them without removing it.

If spokes are rusted or "frozen" on, remove the wheel and tire and apply some penetrating oil (such as Liquid Wrench) to the nipple. If that doesn't work, go to a bike shop. If only one or two spokes are the problem, cut and replace them.

Deflate the tire when you work on spokes so you won't puncture it. Before you re-inflate it, feel under the tube to check that no spoke ends protrude. If they do, remove the tire and file them off.

To true a wheel: Although simple, this is a tedious and time-consuming process. If the wheel is out of round, not just warped to one side, take it to a bike shop.

1 Spin the wheel and watch it as it passes through the brake shoes to find warp.

2 Holding chalk (or crayon) next to the rim on the side with the warp, spin the wheel so that it marks the bulged area.

3 Working only in the warped area, loosen the spokes that come from the side of the hub on the warped side of the wheel. Start with the spokes in the center of the warp; loosen only a half-turn. Loosen the others less as you move to the ends of the warped area, unless a spoke is obviously too tight.

4 Tighten spokes from the other side of the hub. Again, start at the center of the warp and make no more than half-turns—unless a spoke is obviously very loose.

5 Spin wheel and check warp. Repeat process until the warp is less than $\frac{1}{16}$".

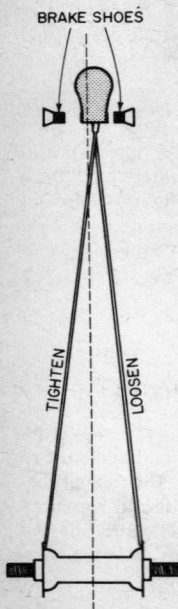

To tighten a loose spoke: Using spoke wrench, alternately tighten the spoke nipple a half-turn and pluck the spoke until it has the same tone as the others or until the same number of threads are showing.

To replace a broken or damaged spoke:* You will need a new spoke the same length and thickness as the others.

1 With spoke wrench, screw spoke out of nipple in rim. If spoke is broken, you may have to hold it with pliers. The rest of the spoke can be pulled out through the hole in the hub, but first, notice which way the spoke goes through.

2 Slide new spoke through hub hole, threaded end first.

3 Observe pattern of spokes and cross spoke correctly.

4 Put spoke into nipple and screw on by hand. Then, tighten like a loose spoke (see above).

* If the spoke is on the sprocket-side of the back wheel: On a derailleur bike, you can remove the freewheel (see p. 58) to get the spoke through the hub hole. But other bikes should be taken to a bike shop, unless your rear sprocket has a hole or slot in it to let a spoke through.

Wheel Troubles

Problem	What to check for
Wheel wiggles.	Loose axle nuts (or quick-release).
	Loose cones in hub.
Wheel binds, won't turn freely.	Tight cones in hub.
	Damaged bearings in hub.
	Hub needs oil or overhaul.
Wheel rubs against brake shoe or fork.	Wheel warped to one side.
	Loose cones.
Regular bumping sound when braking.	Rim is bent.†
Uneven braking.	Wheel warped to one side or out of round.†

† Difficult to repair; best to go to a bike shop.

Index

A

Accessories, 16–17
  baby seats, 18–19
  baskets, 20–21
  bells, 16
  carriers, 20–21
  on children's bikes, 33
  horns, 16
  kickstands, 17
  lights, 78
  locks, 80
  mileage meters, 17
  pumps, 116
  tools, 86–87
  for touring, 127–29
Adjusting a bike:
  handlebars, 72, 74
  seat, 112–13
Adjusting ball bearing
  parts, 95–99
Air pressure, tire, 116
  gauge, 87, 116
  table, 116
Ankling, 106

B

Baby seats, 18–19
Ball bearings, overhauling
  and adjusting, 95–99
Banana seats, 35
Baskets, 20–21
Battery lights, 79
Bearing parts, 95–99
Bells, 16
Bicycle, buying a, 7
Bicycle size, 7
Bicycles, types, 6–15
Blowouts, 117
Bottom bracket, 98–99
Brakes, 22–29
  adjustment, 24–27
  hand-operated, 22–28
  pedal-operated, 29
  problems, 28
Braking, 103
Brazing, 43

Buses:
  riding near, 38
  taking bikes by, 130
Buying a bike, 7

C

Cables:
  brake, 27
  derailleur, 54
  hub gear, 65–67
  maintenance, 90–91
Cadence, pedaling, 107
Cage, derailleur, 46, 56–57
Caliper brakes, 22–28
Camelback frame, 44
Camping by bike, 123
  equipment, 129
Car, taking a bike by, 137
Carriers, 20–21
  for a child, 18–19
  car, 137
Center-pull brakes, 23–28
Chain guards, 31
Chaining a bike, 80–81
Chain length, determining
  on derailleur bike, 59
Chain rivet tool, 59, 87
Chains:
  on derailleur bikes, 59
  on single and 3-speed
   bikes, 30–31
Chain stays, 42
Chainwheel, see Sprockets
Changing a tire, 118–19
Child, carrying a, 18
Children:
  bikes for, 32–35
  teaching to ride, 76–77
City riding, 36–39
Cleaning a bike, 85, 89–93
Clincher tires, 114–20
Clothing:
  for cycling, 40
  for touring, 128
Coaster brakes, 29
Commuting by bike, 36–39

Cones, adjusting, 96—99
Convertible bikes, 34
Cotter pins, 99
Country riding, 124
Cranks:
cottered, 99
cotterless, 99
one-piece, 98
three-piece, 99
Crown, fork, 45
Cyclometer, 17

D

Derailleur bikes, 10—13, 35
Derailleur gears, 10, 46—61
adjusting, 52—59
maintaining, 52—53, 90
troubles, 60—61
using, 49—51
Diamond frame, 44
Dished wheel, 133
Dogs, handling, 125
Dropouts, 45
Dropped handlebars, 72—73
Double-butted tubing, 42
Down tube, 42

E–F

English bikes, 8—9, 35
Fenders, 134
Fifteen-speed bikes, 10, 13, 126
Fifteen spead gears, 47—48
Five-speed bikes, 10—11
Five-speed gears, 46—48
Flat handlebars, 73
Flat tires, 117—20
Folding bikes, 14
Foot position, 106
Forks, 45
Frame construction, 42—43
Frame repair, 43
Frame shapes, 44
Frame size, 7, 42—43
Frame tubes, 42

Freewheels, 46
cleaning, 53
removing, 58
Front changer, 46—47, 55

G

Gear numbers and ratios, 68—71
table, 70
Gear range:
derailleur, 47, 70
three-speed, 64
Gears:
derailleur, 46—61
hub (3-speed), 62—67
Generator lights, 79
Getting on a bike, 108
Grease, 85, 97
Gum-wall tires, 115

H

Handlebars, 72—75
adjusting, 74—75
hand positions on, 105
taping, 75
types, 73
Handlebar bag, 127
Hand levers, brake, 23, 26
Hand-operated brakes, 22—28
Hand positions, 105
Headset, 98
Head tube, 42
Headwear, safety, 41
High-rise bikes, 35
High-rise handlebars, 35, 73
Horns, 16
Hostels, 123
Hub (changer) gears, 3-speed, 9, 62—67
adjusting, 65—67
modifying, 64
range, 64
using, 63
Hubs, 98, 135

I—J—K
Inflating a tire, 116
Intersections, 37—38, 109
Jockey roller, 46
Kickstands, 17

L
Leaks, tire, 117, 120
Learning to ride, 76—77
Left turns, 38
Lights, 78—79
Locks, 80—81
Loop-spring seat, 111
Lubricants, 85
Lugs, 42—43

M
Maes handlebars, 73
Maintenance, 82—99
    guide to, 88—93
    routine, 82, 88—93
Master link, 30—31
Mattress seat, 110
Mechanical tips, 84
Metal pedals, 100—1
Metric parts, 84
Metric tools, 87
Middleweight bikes, 15, 34
Mileage meter, 17
Mirrors, 17
Mixte frame, 44
Mounting a bike, 108

N
Narrow seats, 110—111
Night, riding at, 78

O
Odometer, 17
Oils and oiling, 85—93
Open frame, 44
Overhauling, 95

P
Pace, pedaling, 107
Pannier bags, 127

Parking a bike, 80
Parts of a bike, 142
Patching a tube, 120
Pedaling, 106—7
Pedal-operated brakes, 29
Pedals, 100—1
    overhauling, 98
Plane, taking a bike by, 130
Presta air valve, 121
Pumps, air, 116
Punctures, tire, 117

Q
Quality, bike, 6
Quick-release brakes, 24,
    26
Quick-release hubs, 134

R
Racing seat, 110—11
Rainwear, 41
Raised handlebars, 72—73
Rake of fork, 45
Randonneur handlebars,
    73, 126
Rattrap pedals, 100—1
Reflective belts and vests,
    41
Reflective tape, 78—79
Reflectors, 79
Repairs, complex, 94
Riding:
    in the city, 36—39
    in the country, 124
    learning to, 76—77
    with a load, 125
    at night, 78
Riding positions, 104—5
Riding safety rules, 109
Riding techniques, 102—9
    when touring, 124
Rim brakes, 22—28
Rims, 132—33, 137
Road surface, 39, 108
Rubber pedals, 100—1
Rush hour, 39, 78

S
Saddle bags, 127
Saddles, see Seats
Safety, 109
Safety wear, 41
Seat post, 112–13
Seats, 110–13
    adjusting, 112–13
    types, 110–11
Seat stays, 42
Seat tube, 42
Sew-up tires, 121
Shifting gears:
    derailleur, 49–51
    three-speed, 63
Shoes for cycling, 40
Side-pull brakes, 22–25
Sidewalk bikes, 34
Size, bike, 7
Solvents, 85
Speed:
    calculating, 68–71
    table, 71
    for 3-speed, 64
Speedometers, 17
Spokes, 132–33, 136–37
Sprockets:
    on derailleur bikes, 46–
        48, 58
    on single- and 3-speed
        bikes, 30–31
Stays, 42
Steering, 108
Stem, handlebar, 72–74
Storing a bike, 83

T
Taping handlebars, 75
Tandems, 15
Ten-speed bikes, 10–13
Ten-speed gears, 47–48
Tension roller, 46
Three-speed bikes, 8–9
Three-speed gears, 62–67
Tires, 114–121
    changing, 118–19

Tires (cont.):
    clincher, 114–20
    inflating, 116
    problems, 117
    tubular (sew-up), 121
Toe clips and straps, 100,
    106, 126
Tools, 86–87
    tire, 87, 117
    for touring, 128
Top tube, 42
Touring, 122–29
    equipment for, 126–29
Touring bags, 127
Tourist bike, 8–9
Tourist handlebars, 73
Track bike, 15
Trailers, bike, 20
Train, taking a bike by, 130
Transporting a bike, 130–
    31
Tricycles, adult, 15
Trouble-shooting charts:
    brake, 28
    derailleur, 60–61
    wheel, 137
Truing a wheel, 136
Tubular tires, 121
Turned-down handlebars,
    72–73
Types of bicycles, 6–15

V–W
Valves, tire, 120–21
    Presta, 121
Waxing a bike, 85
Weight of bikes, 6–15
    for touring, 126
Wheels, 132–37; see also
    Tires
    problems, 137
    repairing, 134–37
    truing, 136
Wheel size, 7, 133
    on children's bikes, 32
Wired-on tires, 114–20

Parts and Terms

Parts

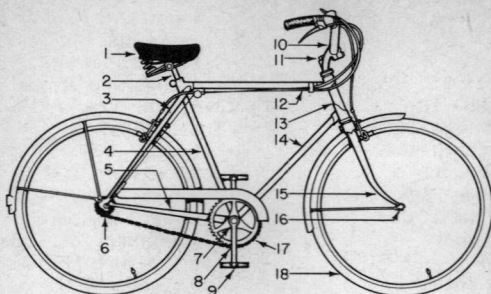

1 Seat (saddle)
2 Seat post
3 Seat stay
4 Seat tube
5 Chain stay
6 Rear sprocket and rear
hub
7 Bottom bracket
8 Crank
9 Pedal

10 Handlebars
11 Stem
12 Top tube
13 Head tube (headset)
14 Down tube
15 Fork
16 Front hub
17 Front sprocket (chain-
wheel)
18 Rim of wheel

Terms

Ankling   A pedaling technique for maximum efficiency.
Cage   The part of the rear derailleur with two rollers that
carries the chain.
Calipher brakes   Another name for hand brakes; rim brakes.
Center-pull brakes   A type of hand brakes (p. 22).
Chainwheel   Front chain sprocket(s).
Clincher tires   Conventional tires. See Wired-ons.
Coaster brakes   Brakes in rear hub operated by back pedal-
ing.
Cotter pin   Wedge-shaped bolt that holds crank on.
Crown   The upper part of the fork where the two blades of
the fork are joined.
Cyclometer   A mileage meter. Odometer.
Derailleur   A mechanism for shifting the chain from one

sprocket to another to change gear ratio.

Dished wheel   Rear wheel with spokes more angled on nongear side than on gear side to center it on bike.

Dropouts   The slots the axles of the wheels fit into.

Freewheel   A rear sprocket that frees from wheel to permit coasting, especially the multiple sprockets on a derailleur.

Headset   All the parts inside the head tube of the frame.

Hubchanger or hub gears   Variable gears inside the hub of the rear wheel. The kind used on 3-speed bikes.

Jockey roller   Upper roller on rear derailleur changer.

Lug   A metal sleeve joining the tubes of the frame.

Master link   A removable chain link that joins the chain into a continuous belt on all bikes except derailleurs.

Mudguard   Fender.

Pannier bags   Saddle bags that fit over the rear wheel.

Presta valve   European air valve used on tubular tires.

Quick-release hubs   Hubs which have a lever-controlled skewer passing through them so the wheel can be removed easily.

Rattrap pedals   Metal racing-style pedals.

Rim   The circular metal part of the wheel that holds tire.

Sew-ups   Narrow racing tires with sewn-in inner tubes.

Side-pull brakes   Most common type of hand brakes.

Sprocket   Metal disk with teeth that the chain passes over.

Stay   Any one of the small tubes that hold the rear wheel.

Steering head   Headset.

Stem   The neck-like post that holds the handlebars.

Tension roller   Lower roller on the rear derailleur changer.

Toe clips   Cage-like devices on metal pedals that hold the ball of the foot on the pedal. Usually used with toe straps.

Touring/tourist   Both terms are overused. But "tourist" usually means "conventional"—a tourist bike is a 3-speed and tourist handlebars are raised handlebars. "Touring" originally referred to long distance racing but is now also used to mean "suited for a long trip"—a touring bike is a derailleur bike suitable for long distance travel and touring handlebars are any square-shaped dropped ones.

Truing   Straightening a wheel by adjusting spokes.

Tubular tires   Narrow racing tires with sewn-in inner tubes.

Turned downs   Dropped handlebars.

Wired-ons   Conventional tires with separate inner tube held on by the tension of internal wire. Clincher tires.

Handlebars
TYPES · ADJUSTING

Learning to Ride
FOR ADULTS AND CHILDREN

Lights
TYPES · SAFE NIGHT RIDING

Locking your Bike
CHAINS AND LOCKS

Maintenance and Repair
CARE · REPAIR · OVERHAULS

Pedals
TYPES · FIXING · REPLACING

Riding Techniques
RIDING WELL SAFELY

Seats
TYPES · POSITION · ADJUSTING

Tires
TYPES · FILLING · CHANGING

Touring by Bike
PLANNING · EQUIPMENT

Transporting a Bike
BY BUS, PLANE, OR CAR

Wheels
FIXING · ADJUSTING

Index
IF NOT ABOVE, LOOK HERE

Parts and Terms
A SHORT DICTIONARY

CREDITS: Many thanks to Mrs. Virginia Garvey and Raleigh Industries of America for the art on pp. 12, 21, 53, 95, 105, and 142; to the Bicycle Institute of America for the silhouettes on pp. 44 and 73; to Shimano for p. 54; to Mafac for p. 87; and to the manufacturers identified for pp. 56–57. In most cases, the art was relabeled or modified.